MOTION PICTURES

The Instructional Media Library

Volume Number 8

MOTION PICTURES

LaMond F. Beatty
Educational Systems and Learning Resources
University of Utah

James E. Duane
Series Editor

Educational Technology Publications
Englewood Cliffs, New Jersey 07632

Library of Congress Cataloging in Publication Data

Beatty, LaMond F
    Motion pictures.

    (The Instructional media library ; v. no. 8)
    Bibliography: p.
    1. Moving-pictures in education. I. Title.
II. Series: Instructional media library ; v. no. 8.
LB1044.B36   371.3'3523   80-21340
ISBN 0-87778-168-0

Printed in the United States of America.

Library of Congress Catalog Card Number:
80-21340

International Standard Book Number:
0-87778-168-0

First Printing: January, 1981.

Table of Contents

MOTION PICTURES

1.

Introduction

On a bright, sunny afternoon, when the angle of reflection is just right, the sun's rays will shine through a window and cast an image of a tree or a bush on an inside wall. Many centuries ago, an ingenious person observed this same phenomenon and invented the "magic lantern." This lantern was the first attempt to project still pictures using sunlight at first, then oil, kerosene, gas, and finally, electricity as a source of illumination. With improvement of the optical system of lenses and reflectors, and by using square, circular, and oblong pieces of oiled paper, glass, film, and plastic as slides, the simple magic lantern has evolved into the many types of projection equipment utilized in education today.

It has been the desire of ingenious men for many centuries to make still pictures move. From the pictographs on cave walls in France to the discovery, in 1824, by Peter Mark Roget, of the capability of the retina of the human eye to retain an image for a short time after the stimulus for the image has disappeared—called persistence of vision—man has invented a host of gadgets, including peep-hole devices, revolving drums, flipping cards, and other devices designed to enable the viewer to see pictures that presented the *appearance* of movement.

One of the simplest forms of these devices was a stick attached to a piece of stiff disc-shaped paper with a bird painted on one side and a bird cage on the other side. This device was called a *thaumathrope;* see Figure 1. When revolved in the hand, the bird appeared to be in the cage, much to the delight of the viewer.

Motion pictures that moved, with any degree of realism, became possible with the development of practical photography. Many dedicated persons made the 16mm motion picture possible.

Thomas Edison invented machines that led to the final perfection of the motion picture projector. George Eastman's introduction of flexible film, capable of passing through the intricacies of the motion picture projector, was also a giant step in development. Other inventors that helped were August and Louis Lumiere of France (1894), who developed a machine that would not only expose motion picture film negatives but also would print the negatives and project them as well. The Lumieres' *Cinematograph* used a pull-down claw, activated by a triangular intermittent cam to advance the film. During 1894-1896, the Lumiere Brothers were active in film production. Robert Paul of England developed a motion picture projector which he sold to several countries around the world, thereby spreading the use of motion picture projectors and films. During 1895-1896, he was actively engaged in the projection of "trick" and "chase" motion picture films. Thomas Armat of the United States contributed to the development of the intermittent method of moving film in front of the aperture opening to project one frame of film. His invention, called the *Phantascope,* was a forerunner of the modern-day motion picture projector. The final great contributor to the development of the 16mm motion picture projector and 16mm film was C.E.K. Mees of the Eastman Kodak Company. In January, 1923, Dr. Mees introduced a practical projector and reversible film to the film industry and thereby provided the impetus for the refinement and further development of portable projectors

Figure 1

*Device (thaumathrope) for illustrating
persistence of vision.*

and 16mm safety film. This made motion pictures available in the educational, industrial, and religious fields.

In 1926, the Warner Brothers Vitaphone system, which coupled a record synchronized with film, was introduced to the theatrical film industry. With this important contribution, sound motion pictures were introduced to the world. It wasn't until 1930, however, that this system was adapted to 16mm motion picture films. In 1932, Radio Corporation of America perfected the optical sound-on-film method, replacing the Vitaphone system. With this development of sound-on-film, the continued development of film (Kodachrome film was introduced in 1935), and the perfection of portable motion picture projectors, the 16mm motion picture came of age as an important tool in the education of students and trainees in classrooms throughout the world.

Today educators and students have at their disposal thousands of educational films designed specifically for classroom use in small-group, large-group, and individualized study. Today motion picture films are available in all subject areas.

These motion picture films enable the classroom teacher to re-create in the classroom actions, events, happenings, processes, or occasions taking place anywhere in the world. People, places, and things from all lands can become real experiences for students in the classroom, without the handicaps of distance, or physical or time barriers. Happenings on the other side of the world, at the top of the earth, in outer space, inside other planets, and even within the human or animal body can be explored in depth and detail. The ancient history of man, the earth, and space can be explored; items too small to see with the unaided human eye can be seen; and the future can be presented through the sound motion picture projector and sound film.

Objectives

After completing this book, the reader will be able to:

- Suggest several purposes for using a 16mm film as part of an instructional unit.
- Describe 16mm film format including the size of each frame, the three layers that comprise film, how the sound track is made, and how a 16mm projector reproduces the sound track.
- Describe the activities a teacher should complete before using a 16mm sound film in the classroom.
- List several methods of preparing a class of students to view and listen to a sound 16mm film presentation.

- Explain and defend the importance of introducing the 16mm sound film lesson, developing class readiness, and leading follow-up activities after viewing the film.

2.

Description of the Medium

There are three sizes of motion picture film in common use today: (1) 35mm film, used for filmstrips and for theatrical films; (2) 16mm film, used almost exclusively for public and private educational purposes; and (3) 8mm and Super 8mm film, used for educational purposes and for amateur home photography.

All 16mm motion picture film stock is manufactured with a film base made of cellulose-acetate. This base will not catch fire or burn and is not explosive. It is called a "safety-film." The 16mm film consists of three parts: (1) the cellulose-acetate base which comprises most of the thickness of the film and is the *shiny* side; (2) the emulsion, consisting of a gelatine substance in which the picture image is formed and is the *dull* side of the film; and (3) the binder, which is a thin layer of glue used to hold the emulsion to the base. Figure 2 illustrates these three parts of film stock.

In black and white film, the images are formed of silver nitrate, and in color films, they are formed of vegetable and chemical dyes. All of the picture image agents are contained in the emulsion portion of the film.

The 16mm sound motion picture film is exactly 16 millimeters wide, with an actual picture dimension of 10mm wide by 7½mm high. The remaining 6mm of the film width is utilized for the sprocket holes and the sound track, each

Figure 2

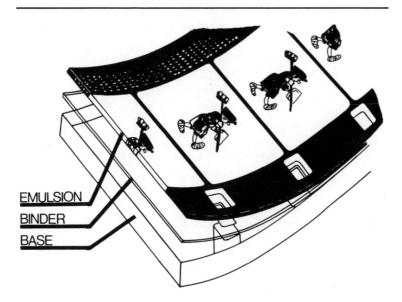

The three parts that
comprise photographic film.

3mm wide. Each individual picture is called a frame. A motion picture film is made up of thousands of these individual frames. A running foot of film contains 40 frames; thus, a film of 360 feet with a playing time of 10 minutes would contain 14,400 individual frames.

A 16mm motion picture film runs at 24 frames per second in sound speed and 16 frames per second in silent speed. This means a sound film travels through a projector at 36 feet per minute, while silent film moves at 24 feet per minute (see Figure 3).

Motion picture film is mounted on reels of different sizes, according to the length of the film. The 400-foot reel is considered to be "one reel," other sizes are increments of

Figure 3

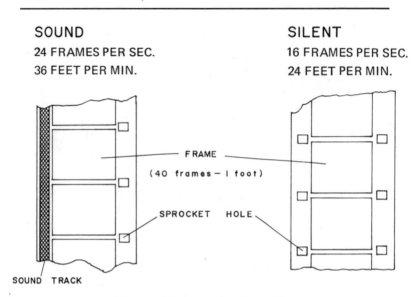

SOUND	SILENT
24 FRAMES PER SEC.	16 FRAMES PER SEC.
36 FEET PER MIN.	24 FEET PER MIN.

FRAME

(40 frames — 1 foot)

SPROCKET HOLE

SOUND TRACK

Sixteen millimeter motion picture film,
sound and silent, formats.

this; i.e., 800 feet equal two reels, 1,200 feet equal three reels, 1,600 feet equal four reels, and 2,000 feet equal five reels, the largest sized reel possible in 16mm film. One reel is considered to average 11 minutes running time, even though a reel may actually contain anywhere from 250 to 400 feet of film. Thus, one reel (400 feet) will run approximately 11 minutes; two reels, 22 minutes; three reels, 33 minutes; four reels, 44 minutes; and five reels, 55 minutes. (See Figure 4.)

The illusion of motion is created when a series of many still pictures flashes rapidly on a screen. The retina of the human eye is able to retain an image for a short time after the stimulus for the image has disappeared—called persistence of vision—if the sequence of pictures has a slight variation in each frame. Thus, if a series of illustrations is photographed so

Figure 4

16MM REEL SIZE — RUNNING TIME — SOUND SPEED

FEET OF FILM	REEL	MINUTES
400	I	II
800	2	22
I, 200	3	33
I, 600	4	44
2, 000	5	55

16mm motion picture film is mounted on reels of several sizes. The 400-foot reel is considered "one-reel"; other sizes are increments of this; thus, the 800-foot reel is "two-reels"; and so on. The table above shows the relationship of film footage, reel size, and showing time.

each image is in a slightly different position (see Figure 5) from the preceding one and then projected at 24 frames per second, the viewer will have the impression of continual motion.

Each picture must stay on the screen for a short duration in order to provide the effect of continuous motion. The film does not pass by the projector aperture evenly—each frame stops briefly in front of the aperture. The film movement is an intermittent or jerky motion in this area of the projector. The motion picture projector has a mechanism called the "intermittent device" or "intermittent claw" that moves the film into position to expose one frame, holds it in a fixed position for an instant, and then moves on to the next frame.

A viewer would not be able to watch a motion picture if it were merely a series of still pictures passing by on a screen,

Figure 5

Illusion of motion on 16mm film.

When a series of illustrations is placed on a strip of film so that each image is in a slightly different position from the preceding one and then projected in rapid succession by a motion picture projector, an illusion of motion is created.

one after another, in a jerky fashion. The lines between the frames, combined with the intermittent movement, would create a flicker for which no psychological persistence of vision could compensate.

To eliminate the flicker during projection, a shutter is utilized in the motion picture projector. The shutter cuts off the light for the split second it takes the intermittent claw to move the next frame into position. The duration the light is blocked by the shutter is so short that because of the marvel of persistence of vision, the viewer never notices that the light has been off and on, again and again, 24 times per second. Figure 6 illustrates a simplified "projection section" of the motion picture projector with a description of each part that comprises this section.

About all 16mm films shown today have sound in addition to motion. The sound track, either optical or magnetic, is contained on the side of the film opposite the sprocket holes (refer to Figure 3). The sound track portion for any given frame is recorded exactly 26 frames ahead of the picture frame. This is done so that the appropriate part of the sound track will pass over the sound drum at the same instant the picture is passing by the light aperture. The picture is projected on the screen, and the sound is reproduced by the loudspeaker simultaneously. The exact 26-frame spacing between the picture in the aperture and the sound on the sound drum is controlled by the extent of the lower loop under the aperture opening. If the loop is too short or too long, as designated and indicated on the face of the projection machine by the manufacturer, the sound and picture will not be in synchronization.

It is very distracting to viewers to have the actor's lips move, with his words coming from the loudspeaker either before or after the movement. This lack of synchronization can be corrected by properly adjusting the lower loop.

The sound for a 16mm motion picture film is photo-

Figure 6

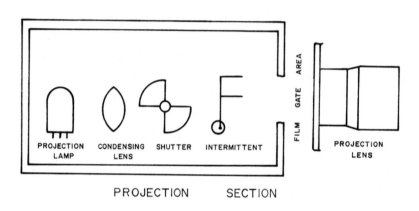

PROJECTION   SECTION

The Projection Section consists of:

Projection Lamp—source of light for the projection section of the 16mm projector.

Condensing Lens—concentrates/condenses the light into a small beam that will pass through the aperture opening.

Shutter—device that acts as the "on" and "off" switch to control the passing of light through the aperture opening.

Intermittent—device that moves one frame of the film in front of the aperture opening.

Film Gate Area—area where film is clamped or locked to facilitate projection of one frame of the film.

Projection Lens—transparent substance with curved surfaces used to create images on a projection screen by bending light rays.

graphed on film or recorded on an iron oxide strip adhered to the photographic film. When the sound is photographed, the sound waves are picked up by a microphone, which converts the varying patterns of sound waves into a similarly varying electric current. These current variations control a *light valve.* The light valve used in some sound recording is composed of two metallic ribbons or diaphragms set in a magnetic field which move apart or together in response to the variations in electric current. A constant beam of light is focused on this valve, and the opening and closing of the valve allow similar light variations to be recorded as light and dark areas on the photographic film.

Some optical sound tracks are produced using a galvanometer, an instrument used to measure electric current. Its mechanism also moves in response to changes or pulsations in the electric current. Fastened to the galvanometer is a mirror. The current pulsations coming from the microphone and amplified by the amplifier cause the mirror to turn back and forth on its axis to the degree that the pulsations vary. A steady, narrow beam of light is shined on the mirror. As the mirror swings back and forth, the light beam will swing with it. This movement is slight, and thus the pattern of light is very precise. Unexposed photographic film is run past this narrow beam of light. The light beam will move in exact correspondence to the original pulsation of the current coming from the microphone. The exposed pattern of light and dark areas on the film becomes the sound track. In magnetic sound track recordings, the oxide coating on the film is magnetized in varying patterns corresponding to the current coming from the microphone.

A sound 16mm motion picture projector contains not only the projection section but also a section that reproduces either a magnetic and/or an optical sound track. Most sound 16mm projectors have only the optical sound system, the optical/magnetic option being found only in specialized machines.

In projection, the jerkiness of the projected film is smoothed out and made regular by constantly turning sprocket wheels and guide rollers. The smoothly flowing film is then passed over a mechanism called the sound drum or sound head, which contains the elements of the system which reproduce the sound.

As the film passes by a tiny slit in the sound drum, light from the exciter lamp is concentrated on the sound track area. The variations of light and dark areas in the sound track cause the light which passes through the film to vary in intensity.

This light passing through the sound track area of the film is reflected into a photo-electric cell, which changes the variations in light energy to corresponding variations of electrical energy—in exactly the same pattern as those picked up by the microphone in the original sound. These electrical current pulsations are then amplified, fed to the loudspeaker, and there converted back into sound. Figure 7 shows a simplified diagram of the "sound section" of the motion picture projector with a description of each part that comprises this section.

Figure 7

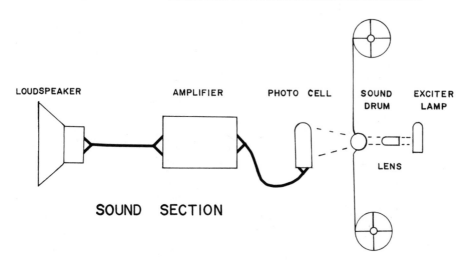

The Sound Section consists of:

Exciter Lamp—source of light for the sound system. Shines light through the sound track of the film.

Lens—concentrates the light from the exciter lamp onto the sound track area of the film.

Sound Drum—device used to stabilize the film. Film passes around two-thirds of the circumference of the sound drum.

Photo Cell—converts light waves/rays into electrical impulses. Senses the varying light patterns coming through the sound track and converts these patterns to varying electrical impulses.

Amplifier—device that boosts up (makes stronger) the electrical impulses coming from the photo cell.

Loudspeaker—device that converts the electrical impulses into sound waves.

3.

Characteristics:
Advantages and Disadvantages

1. Most 16mm motion picture films are sound films. Very few silent films are available, except in the physical sciences area.

2. Sound films and motion picture projectors are relatively expensive. Motion picture projectors require precise threading, need a fairly large area for projection, and necessitate a darkened room for effective large-group viewing.

3. Films are designed primarily for group viewing. However, 16mm films can be used in individualized instruction applications, with special equipment.

4. Film presentations for individualized instruction can be accomplished by utilizing a large, 48-inch by 30-inch, student study carrel and headphones. For small-group instruction, the projector can be set up in a small room or a corner of a classroom, and film can be projected on a small beaded screen or white piece of paper, with the sound coming through headphones connected to a junction box that will accommodate eight to ten sets.

5. Film is classified as having both fixed sequence and fixed pacing. The pacing can be altered by utilizing a "still-frame" projector.

6. Many thousands of individual titles in *all subject areas* are commercially available on 16mm sound/silent film.

7. Sound films cost approximately $75.00 to $600.00 for commercially produced films. Silent commercially produced films range from $37.50 to $300.00. Sound motion picture projectors cost approximately $800.00 per projector. Almost all 16mm motion picture projectors manufactured today are combined sound/silent projectors.

8. All 16mm sound films combine effectively the two assets of high-quality still pictures and sound into a motion format.

9. A portion or all of a sound 16mm film can be repeated either by backing up and re-showing the appropriate section or by rewinding the entire film and re-showing appropriate sections.

10. When instructional media stimuli relationships to learning objectives are considered, sound motion picture films are extremely effective in learning visual identifications, principles, concepts, rules, and procedures. They are not as effective in learning factual information or performing skilled perceptual motor acts.

11. Films can help to overcome intellectual barriers to learning because they depend little upon skills of reading. Students with reading deficiencies can be helped by a well-paced, clearly presented sound film showing moving, dramatic, colorful events that they would not be able to experience through reading.

12. Motion picture films can help re-create the past. Ancient, recent, and current history can be made "real" and "believable" with dramatized films. Because sound films involve viewers, cause them to become a part of the action, and produce highly emotionalized responses, history comes alive for most students.

13. Sound motion picture films can provide a whole class of students with a common experience. They can help bridge background differences for members of the same and differing ethnic groups.

14. When continuity of action occurring in real life is needed, films can provide the step-by-step, minute-by-minute accounting needed to show the world as it actually exists.

15. Special photographic techniques, such as animation, microphotography, macrophotography, telephotography, time-lapse photography, and telescope/space photography, provide ways to overcome many physical limitations to learning and extend the limited range of the normal human senses. Materials too large, too small, invisible, or impossible to see with the human eye; too dangerous to handle and observe; and too expensive to provide in the classroom can be presented to every student via sound films.

16. The motion picture film can control the time factor in operations or series of events. Slow-motion, time-lapse, and high-speed photography make this uniqueness possible.

17. The motion picture film compels sustained attention. In a darkened room, most outside distractions are reduced, and the movement and sound couple to attract and hold the viewer's whole attention.

18. Most motion picture films are an edited version of reality. This editing, which involves the manipulation of time, space, and objects, heightens reality by eliminating distractions and pointing up key relationships.

19. Motion picture films can develop an understanding of abstract relationships. Utilizing a series of pictures, aided by a sound narration, events that took thousands of years to happen can be presented in a matter of minutes. Space can be transcended, and related events joined. Relationships among things and events can be clarified with animated drawings of charts, diagrams, and graphs as well as enhanced with special sound effects.

4.

Utilization

Lesson Planning

An effective lesson with a sound 16mm film has all the ingredients of any well-prepared instructional sequence:

(1) clearly defined purposes/rationale;

(2) precisely stated behavioral objectives/goals;

(3) well-selected instructional materials which give the subject matter clarity, provide reality, and achieve the desired behavioral objective(s);

(4) a lesson plan which moves logically and smoothly from one point to the next;

(5) a well-executed, interesting, student-involved presentation;

(6) follow-up activities commencing immediately after the film presentation to strengthen and extend the learning of the students participating in the lesson; and

(7) evaluation that demonstrates that the behavioral objectives have been achieved.

Purposes

Student needs and interests should determine instructional purposes. Sound motion picture films can stimulate students' interest in new areas of study and can help them organize, review, or summarize currently studied subject matter. Films can introduce a new unit, can visualize and expand a particular subject area, can bring the world into the class-room, and can explain or clarify difficult subjects. Sound films can present skills and processes and can provide background information and facts. They can stimulate emotions, build attitudes, and point out social, psychological, and physical problems. Films re-create effectively events of the past, clarify size, make abstract concepts more tangible, increase student motivation, and stimulate further study in diverse or parallel subject areas.

Many 16mm sound films are correlated to textbooks currently being used in public schools, thereby providing enrichment and clarification of the printed word.

Students are helped by films in the development of concept formation involving the application of discrimination skills, along with generalizing skills, both of which are highly dependent upon encounters with sensory phenomena. In order for basic concepts to be formed, it is necessary that students have direct encounters with the elements that make up the concept. Sound motion pictures can provide such basic elements.

Selection

When selecting a 16mm motion picture film for use in a particular lesson, choose one which comes as close as possible to meeting student-teacher objectives, purposes, needs, and interests. The appropriateness of the film to meet these needs can be assessed by answering the following questions:

1. Is it well-organized?
2. Will it be interesting and stimulating to the students?
3. Are the facts presented up-to-date and accurate?
4. Are presentation methods, styles of dress shown, real objects presented, historical events depicted, and filming techniques utilized appropriate?
5. If there are graphs, posters, charts, diagrams, superim-

posed words, etc., included in the film, are they clear, sharp, and appropriate for the subject matter presented?

6. Does the content fit the age level and experience of the group who will use it?
7. Are the materials presented in a logical sequence?
8. Will the 16mm film encourage student involvement and stimulate critical thinking?

Planning and Presenting the Lesson

There is no one best way of teaching with motion picture films. A great deal of the success of the lesson depends upon the purposes the teacher has in mind, the physical conditions, the appropriateness of the films themselves, and the readiness of the students for the materials presented. For most situations, however, a generalized methodology for planning and presenting lessons should include the following six steps:

1. Prepare yourself.
2. Prepare environment and projection equipment.
3. Prepare students.
4. Present media.
5. Prepare follow-up activities.
6. Prepare evaluation (student and teacher).

1. Prepare Yourself

It is absolutely essential that users of motion picture films preview them before any class showing. A teacher will increase a film's value to students by becoming thoroughly familiar with it. A teacher is not able to determine the appropriateness of a film to achieve the desired objective(s) just by looking at the title and reading a brief annotation in a film catalog or on top of the film can. A thorough examination of the entire motion picture film is a MUST. The careful previewing of the film will:

a. Point up for special emphasis scenes to which students

should pay special attention in order to achieve the objec-
tive(s) for the lesson.

b. Note vocabulary words that should be explained before
the class sees the film.

c. Create questions to guide students' viewing of the film.
These questions could be written on the chalkboard, a chart,
an overhead transparency, or printed on hand-out sheets and
given to the students.

d. Note any inaccuracies of fact or pictorial content and
biased views presented in the film, which should be discussed
and balanced with different viewpoints.

e. Point up any special film techniques that need to be
clarified for students before seeing the film. Animated
sequences, time-lapse portions, high-speed photography sections, etc., may not seem real to some students. A brief
explanation of these techniques will help create the illusion
of reality.

f. Determine whether a sponsored film emphasizes "to an
extreme" the product or idea of the industry or organization
that produced it. In judging this aspect of sponsored films,
considerations for determining the educational value might
include the following items:

- To what degree do the objectives of the motion
  picture film harmonize with the educational objectives of the school?
- Does the material present general understanding,
  facts, processes, or methods, or does it present a
  particular point of view or promote a specific
  brand/product?
- To what extent is the material sound in terms of
  educational philosophy?
- Is one point of view stressed in an obviously
  two-sided issue?
- Does it present major emphasis on negative, rather
  than positive, aspects of the issue?

- To what extent is the sponsor's relationship to the film clearly known and acceptably stated?

g. Point up any datedness of the film so that an explanation of the value of the content versus the datedness of dress, hair style, automobiles, etc., can be made. A brief explanation to students in preparation for what they are about to see concerning this aspect of the film will help eliminate distractions caused by unfamiliar styles of dress, old vehicles, etc. *Remember:* an old film may teach as well as a new one; content is the key to the usefulness of the film.

The previewing of motion picture films is a time-consuming process. Manufacturers of projectors do not produce an economically priced machine that will show a film at speeds faster than 24 frames per second; consequently, a film with a running time of 20 minutes will take longer than 20 minutes to preview effectively.

A teacher should always use a "preview" form when preparing a film for classroom use. This form should include space to record all the pertinent data needed to introduce the film lesson to the class plus vital data for re-ordering and reviewing the film when needed next term, next semester, or next year. An adequate preview form must include at least the following components:

(1) space for listing objective(s);

(2) space for a description of content (synopsis);

(3) space to include a section for listing potential or actual contributions to the achievement of the objective(s);

(4) space to include sources of additional materials that will enhance the film presentation;

(5) space for a description of the physical quality;

(6) space for special characteristics of materials displayed in the film; and

(7) space for a vocabulary list.

Figure 8 shows a sample preview form.

Figure 8

FILM EVALUATION FORM

Title_____Producer_____

Type of Material_____ Running Time_____ Color_____ Black and White_____ Date Previewed_____

Source_____ Production Date_____ Series_____

---

1. Subject or Major Concepts_____

2. Please check (ı) school levels for which material is appropriate. Double check (ı ı) most appropriate school level:

    Primary_____ Intermediate_____ Junior High/Upper_____ High School_____ College_____ Teacher Ed._____

3. How does the material relate to the curriculum? _____ Basic_____ Enrichment_____ None_____

4. Is this medium a suitable way to present this subject or concept?   Yes_____ Undecided_____ No_____

5. Is the information presented authentic and accurate? _____ Yes_____ Questionable_____ No_____

6. Is the production technically good? (If "no" please give reason on back) _____ Yes_____ No_____

7. Is color essential to understanding? _____ Essential_____ Non-essential_____

8. Would you recommend this material for use at the appropriate school levels? Yes_____ Uncertain_____ No_____

Name_____Title_____

Organization_____City_____

COMMENTS

Denote significance_____
_____
_____
_____

Denote uniqueness_____
_____
_____
_____

Denote weakness_____
_____
_____
_____

Comment on technical quality_____
_____
_____
_____

Film Evaluation Form, courtesy of the Educational Media Center,
University of Utah, Salt Lake City, Utah.

As has been previously mentioned, previewing is a time-consuming process. Some suggestions to help improve the effectiveness of the previewing session are as follows:

- Use a projector that can be stopped easily and the film backed up for re-showing. A "stop-on-frame" capability is desirable, allowing the teacher to stop the film on any one frame for extended viewing and note-taking.
- Observe the initial scenes carefully. In an educational film, these first few scenes outline what is to follow.
- Record key words presented in the film rather than trying to write whole sentences.
- Record vocabulary words in order of presentation. This is the easiest method of recording the film outline.
- When a fade-out and then a fade-in are presented, this indicates a new point in the film outline.
- A partial summary of content indicates a new point is coming up in the film.
- Record all superimposed words or phrases and basic information on maps, charts, diagrams, posters, etc.
- The synopsis, recorded on the preview form, should be an outline of the film content, without any value judgments. The synopsis is used to introduce the film content to students.
- The review that often comes at the end of the film will summarize the key elements in the film content. Pay special attention to this summary to check whether any points were missed.
- Strong and weak areas of the preview form are also used for USE suggestions.

Small, desk-top 16mm sound viewers are not available; consequently, the same machine used to project the film in the regular classroom must also be used for previewing purposes; see Figure 9. Teachers preview films in the regular

Figure 9

*Teacher previewing a 16mm film in preparation for classroom utilization. Photo
courtesy of the Educational Media Center, University of Utah.*

classroom, in small preview rooms, or in their offices. The
image can be projected on a small screen or on a white card.
The sound can come either from the loudspeaker of the
projector or be heard through earphones. Teachers usually
preview films before or after regular class periods and during
their preparation periods. As this is valuable, limited time,
correct previewing techniques as outlined above are essential
for effective utilization of these periods.

The teacher may do the previewing alone; however, it is
often advantageous to utilize a committee of classroom
students with this phase of teacher preparation, and the
involvement of students in the preview session provides an
opportunity for them to become part of the planning and
presentation of the lesson. Students could lead the introduc-

tion and discussion of the film lesson plus serve as the chairpersons of the follow-up study groups.

During the preview session, a teacher should note the organization of the film content and prepare an outline of the main points presented. This outline should include: (1) behavioral objective(s); (2) pretest, if desired; (3) key vocabulary words; (4) some questions that will be answered by the film presentation; (5) follow-up activities; and (6) posttest or evaluation.

As the teacher previews the film, ideas for other resources necessary to supplement the information presented should be noted on the preview form. These additional resources could include such items as maps, reference books, magazines and other printed materials, overhead transparencies, flat pictures, wall charts, chalkboard illustrations, diagrams, mimeographed hand-outs, models, and real objects. The actual collection of these resources can be facilitated greatly by the "preview-session" students. They can be assigned the task of locating and preparing these items, thereby directly involving them and freeing the teacher to assist in other ways. Many teachers find it appropriate to have students take the full responsibility for selecting, previewing, introducing, leading the classroom presentation, making follow-up demonstrations, and leading study groups.

Motion picture film-makers use a great variety of production techniques to produce effective teaching films. Teachers, students, and all other users of motion picture films need to be familiar with the different types available to them. Any classification system will result in some overlapping; however, the following types of films and the photographic techniques used are relatively discrete and useful to teachers in classifying films.

Documentary—films specializing in the realistic and factual treatment of a subject without the benefit of professional actors/actresses and contrived stage settings. Documentary films try to tell true, accurate, edited stories about real-life situations and people.

Travelogue—films which present geographical information about towns, cities, counties, states, nations, regions, continents, rivers, lakes, oceans, etc.

Direct—Real-Life—films which use the camera and microphone to record and present events precisely as they occur, with little or no editing.

Drama—Fictional—films which present believable expositions of literary works. These films make literary works understandable, build appreciation, and assist in developing attitudes. Generally, these films present edited versions of the literary works.

Drama—True-Life—films which depict events in the lives of real people. These are generally edited versions of real events. They re-create the lives of people, usually against a background embodying the social and political conditions of the period in which they lived.

Religious—films which emphasize religious history or events and dramatize occurrences involving moral and spiritual values. These films may also have as a theme the life of a religious leader along with the events of his or her period of history.

Sponsored—films produced by a business or industrial firm for the purpose of informing the viewer about the company and its many products. Most of these films are part of the public relations effort of the company and, as such, are distributed to the user free-of-charge, except for the transportation costs necessary to receive and return the film.

Microphotography—also termed *photomicrography*—a photographic technique which requires a special camera attached to a microscope with a lighting apparatus that provides enough light to record the microscopic images on film. Microphotography provides the capability of demonstrating activities of organisms too small to be seen except by means of some highly magnified device. Micro-organisms never seen by human eyes can be photographed using an electron microscope and a special camera and then projected on a large screen in a classroom for students to examine in detail. This technique affords students the opportunity to observe the motion of single blood cells moving through the capillaries, the process of cell division, the action of a white blood cell attacking bacteria, the growth and multiplication of amoebae, etc.

Slow-Motion Photography—a technique utilizing a special camera which takes more frames per second than the motion picture projector ordinarily plays back. Because these additional frames take longer to run through the projector, the actual action appears to take longer, thus giving the effect of slow motion. This technique, especially in sports endeavors, permits the viewer to see the precise movements slowly enough to analyze individual elements of the total performance, i.e., a tennis serve, kicking a football, an intricate dive, pitching a baseball, etc.

Time-Lapse Photography—a technique requiring an intricate lighting arrangement and a special camera that takes single pictures at regular intervals (one every 30 seconds, or one every minute, hour, etc.) over an extended period of time. When these frames are projected on the motion picture projector at the regular speed of 24 frames per second, a camera which takes one frame per second will speed up the real action 24 times. This technique allows a viewer to see a flower open its petals to receive the sun's rays, to see a bean seed germinate and develop into a mature plant, or to see a wisp of clouds develop into a full-blown storm front—all in a matter of a minute or two of projection time. This action may normally take hours or even days; however, time-lapse photography allows the student/viewer to observe the uniqueness of nature in ways he or she could not economically or physically see any other way.

Animation—a photographic technique which involves a camera that can take one frame at a time. The camera is usually placed on a special copy table called an animation stand. A series of drawings depicting movement is photographed in a sequence that when projected at 24 frames per second gives the illusion of motion. These drawings could be of a cartoon character, a series of maps, charts, diagrams, or posters photographed in a sequence that shows a body movement, a process, or an activity. Each phase of the movement is drawn separately and then the various phases are photographed in proper sequence on motion picture film. Animation provides an opportunity for the viewer to see processes and activities that could not be seen in real life. For example, the complex operation of a jet engine; the separation of the stages of a space rocket; the operation of the human ear, eye, heart, or other internal organs; the life history of the boll weevil; the pollination of plants by insects; etc. Animation also serves to explain and illustrate effectively theories, ideas, and hypotheses. It can be the process by which a concept is visualized, abstract ideas are made more concrete through analogy, or a hypothesis is examined and analyzed.

Macrophotography—a technique using a close-up lens on the camera that has the capability of enlarging small objects. This technique is used to photograph the "small world" of nature. For example, the life cycle of the honey bee; the activities in an ant colony; small creatures in a stream, river, or lake; and plants and animals capable of being seen with the naked eye but better understood when photographed and projected on a large classroom screen. This photographic process affords the viewer the opportunity of observing the wonders of nature in brilliant color and in an enlarged dimension which makes learning enjoyable.

X-Ray Photography—a technique which utilizes the fluoroscope screen of an X-ray machine, ultra-sensitive motion picture film, and a camera with a special lens that can photograph X-rays. In some applications, an electronic image intensifier, which makes the X-ray image more detailed, is used. This process presents a record of actions to the viewer which are ordinarily invisible to the human eye, i.e., pictures showing solid materials like animal or human bones, metals and minerals, and dense tissues of animals like the heart, lungs, or other internal organs. Actual movements and articulations of the skeletal parts of animals, such as knee joints, bird wing movements, snake spinal action, etc., can be shown.

Telescope/Space Photography—a technique which utilizes the telescope, such as the Mount Wilson Observatory reflecting telescope, or a telescopic lens, to bring close the distant objects in the viewer's environment. The surface of the moon; the wary and far distant moose, elk, or antelope on a grassy plain; an eagle nesting high on a craggy cliff; a jet plane making lazy spirals in the sky; or the dangerous fangs of the deadly rattlesnake can be brought into the classroom for all to see and study.

2. Prepare Environment and Projection Equipment

In utilizing 16mm sound films, teachers MUST know how to set up properly the environment and projection equipment. Even though some schools provide student projectionists, it is still essential that teachers know correct procedures so that they can assist where necessary and be self-assured of proper projection of their films.

Differing environmental factors affect the selection of the type of screen surface that should be used. A matte surface—a flat, white surface—is suitable for a square room. This screen is also adequate for small-room or office previewing. A white piece of card-stock presents a matte surface. This screen reflects a wide pattern of light, 30 degrees on both sides of the line of projection. Because of the characteristics of this screen surface, it is suitable for rooms that can be completely darkened. Any ambient light entering the room will reduce the quality of the projected image.

A beaded screen, composed of glass beads adhered to a white surface, is suitable for a long, narrow room. This screen surface reflects a narrower pattern of light than a matte screen, 25 degrees on both sides of the line of projection. This screen is suitable for use in a darkened or semi-darkened room as long as the ambient light entering the room does not shine directly on the surface of the screen.

A lenticular, silver metallic screen is suitable for a room that is difficult to darken. This screen reflects a narrow, but intense, image pattern, 20 degrees on both sides of the line of projection. Ambient light should not be allowed to shine directly on this surface.

See Figure 10 for a graphic illustration of the three screen surface types.

For general classroom use, a screen no smaller than 70 x 70 inches should be used. If the room is larger than 30 x 35 feet, a screen larger than 70 x 70 inches should be used. In rooms where the ambient light can be controlled, the screen should be placed directly in the front-center of the class-room.

When a teacher desires to have students take notes during the film presentation, some ambient light may be allowed into the classroom. One-tenth foot candle permits a student to read a newspaper with some difficulty, but this provides ample light for note-taking. This light should be controlled at the back portion of the room—leaving the front screen area in semi-darkness. Modern 16mm sound equipment projects intense beams of light that generally compensate for any ambient light in the room, except where the light shines directly on the screen surface.

In a room where there is extreme difficulty in controlling

Figure 10

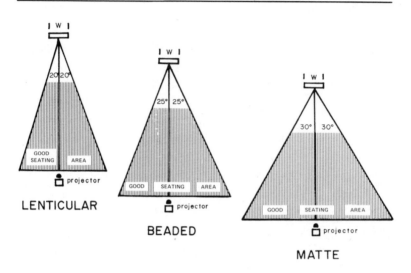

Optimal viewing angles and audience seating areas
for matte, beaded, and lenticular screens.

light, the projection screen should be placed with its back surface toward the light coming from windows, doors, or vents in the room. It may be desirable to move the projector closer to the screen, thereby projecting a smaller, but more intense, beam of light. In this case, the projector will need to be placed in the middle of the room rather than at the back, with students seated around the projector.

The seating arrangement also affects the ability of students to learn from a film lesson. Chairs should be arranged in a wedge-shaped pattern, with the small end toward the front of the room and the wide end at the back. The first row of seats should be no closer than two screen widths and the back row no more than six screen widths from the screen. The bottom of the screen should be at the eye level of the students seated in the classroom.

The motion picture projector should be placed so that the light from the projected beam is clear of obstructions (beam of light is not blocked by a student's head). A projection stand at least 40 inches in height is generally used. The axis of projection must be perpendicular to the screen surface to avoid a "keystoning" effect. Where possible and practical, the projector should be placed so that the projected beam of light fills the entire screen surface. If the projector has a detachable loudspeaker, it should be placed at the front of the room on a desk or table at the ear level of the students in the room.

Full-closure venetian blinds, or the equivalent, are most satisfactory for room darkening. The lighting controls for the room should allow overhead lights to be darkened directly over the projection screen area, while the seating area of the classroom may be partially illuminated. This arrangement allows the taking of notes and the viewing of supplementary materials used in the film presentation.

Adequate room ventilation should be provided when the room is darkened. Air conditioning should provide for adequate movement of air in the room.

The sound motion picture projector should be operated by a person who has received training in the proper care and operation of the machine. Film can be completely destroyed one time through the projector if proper projection procedures are not observed. Sprocket hole damage and scratches in the picture area of the film are the two most common problems associated with poorly trained projectionists. To prevent sprocket hole damage, the following cautions should be observed:

1. Carefully align sprocket holes with the sprocket teeth.
2. Carefully fit the film in the film gate channel.
3. Carefully align the film on the guide rollers, tension rollers, and around the sound drum.

4. Carefully thread the film onto the take-up reel, being sure that the reel is of the correct size and is not bent or damaged in any way.

5. Be sure that the film gate area, sprocket wheels, guide rollers, and sound drum are free of dust, dirt, and accumulated film emulsion. The lenses of the projector should also be cleaned frequently.

3. Prepare Students

Motion picture films often contribute little to student learning because they are shown without proper class preparation. Some teachers feel that because of the uniqueness of films, they do not need much student preparation. Nothing could be further from the truth. When films are "just presented," without a clear understanding of the objectives intended for the lesson, they seldom contribute much to student learning. Learning from an educational film is an acquired skill—much like learning from a textbook. A skillful classroom teacher should perform the following preliminary steps to assure proper preparation:

1. The lesson objectives should be presented and discussed so that students know WHAT they are expected to learn from seeing the film. They need to know what specific bits of information are important to remember; how and on what they will be evaluated; and why this information is of concern to them. The presentation of the lesson objective(s) sets the parameters for the film presentation.

2. Discuss what is already known about the subject of the film. Use this review as a springboard into what is expected from the film presentation.

3. Key words should be presented by listing them on the chalkboard, an overhead transparency, or a chart. Class members MUST become familiar with their meaning before the film presentation. These words could have been the daily or weekly spelling list words, or they could have been used as

key words for compositions, crossword puzzles, spelling or word games, etc. However used, it is important that all students know the words and their meanings prior to the film screening.

4. Develop a list of questions which may be answered by the film. These questions could be listed on the chalkboard, written on an overhead transparency, or printed on paper as a hand-out. The hand-out "guide-to-viewing" technique is an excellent method for focusing the students' attention on the major concepts deemed important in the film. Students could be asked to discuss ways in which the film content agrees or disagrees with their existing knowledge and impressions. They could be asked to evaluate the film technique itself and to appraise the accuracy and adequacy of its treatment of the subject.

5. Students could be assigned to pay special attention to specific sections of the film and then report their findings to the whole class in the follow-up discussion. The students that were members of the "preview session" could be the chairpersons of these discussion groups.

6. Explain the photographic techniques used in the film. Many students are unfamiliar with the effects of time-lapse photography, slow-motion photography, animation, or microphotography. These techniques and the contributions they make to clarifying difficult subjects should be clearly understood by students.

7. Students should be told the exact title of the film and the educational collaborator, if it is the same person who wrote the textbook used in the class.

8. The teacher should indicate whether there will be a follow-up discussion, a committee assignment or individual research project(s), and a written, oral, or some other type of evaluation following the film presentation.

Remember: It is important to make clear to all students WHY they are seeing the film and WHAT they are expected to learn from it. Skillful teachers develop class readiness for seeing films in many different ways. The eight steps listed above can be modified and utilized in differing ways; however, all students learn best when they know the objective(s) of the lesson and participate in careful preparation before seeing the film.

4. Present Media

Most often, teachers show the entire film without interruption. In many films, an interruption may cause a break in thought or the development of concepts which are interrelated. If this is the case, no interruptions should occur. Other times, a teacher may want to show only part of a film. Reasons for this may be that only a small part of the film is relevant to the development of the objective(s), or that a certain sound track does not lend itself to the level or inclination of the class.

Some teachers show a film twice. The first time through, the students watch the film without taking notes or making any comments about content. The second showing is used for note-taking of key content and recording of student impressions. Students often read a textbook chapter more than once—why not see a film more than once?

With certain skill films, it may be useful to stop the film several times to let the students practice the skill. If the "practice session" requires some materials or apparatus, these items should be made available prior to the screening of the film.

Many teachers utilize supplementary materials to emphasize and clarify concepts made in the film. These materials can be shown before the film presentation to introduce these concepts, or they may be used more effectively during the actual screening of the film.

5. Prepare Follow-Up Activities

An immediate discussion of the film, led by the teacher or students, is one of the best ways to fix its content in students' minds. The more they think about the film and discuss it immediately after screening, the more they will learn from it. "What were the major points made in the film?" "How does its content fit in with our current work?"

The discussion relates directly to the questions or main points set up in the *Prepare Students* period. As the students discuss the film content, the teacher can check for misunderstandings, unclear concepts, etc. The students and the teacher can also evaluate the extent to which the objectives for seeing the film were met. Other appropriate follow-up activities might include the following:

- Students may make presentations of specially assigned topics or activities.
- Divide the class into small groups. Have students discuss key elements in the film and prepare written reports of their deliberations.
- Assign additional research to be done on the film topic, either in small groups or on an individual basis.
- Assign several groups to develop a bulletin board, a series of flip charts, maps, posters, or other graphic materials on the film topic.
- Re-show all or part of the film as many times as necessary to clarify key points. This can be done with the whole class, a small group, or by an individual student.
- Ask students how they might improve the film, what parts could be left out, and what parts could have additional emphasis.
- Re-show the film with the sound turned off. Have the students react to the picture portion only. Have students rewrite some sections of the sound narration. This rewritten portion might be recorded on a cassette and substituted for the original sound.

- Have students read a related portion of a textbook, reference book, or journal and compare this treatment of the topic with that of the film. This comparison might also be done between the film and an audiotape presentation, an overhead transparency set, a series of flat pictures, (a) filmstrip(s), or a television program.
- Invite a resource person from the community to visit the classroom to answer questions and present additional information on the topic. If the resource person cannot come to the classroom, go to his or her home or place of business and record his or her comments, or arrange for a *Telelecture* utilizing your local telephone company's services.
- Give a written posttest on the content of the film.
- Give an oral posttest on the content of the film.

6. *Prepare Evaluation (Student and Teacher)*

Teachers have the final and ultimate responsibility for assessing the effectiveness of classroom teaching procedures to change the behavior of students in directions approved by society. When motion picture films are used in these teaching procedures, a teacher must make a continuous effort to evaluate their effectiveness for appropriate changes of student behavior.

Teachers evaluate students in many ways. Some pupils respond best to paper and pencil forms, others to verbal interaction, still others to dramatized situations, such as role playing, sociodrama, or group discussion. No matter how the evaluation is conducted, students MUST be held accountable for lesson content, behavior, and attitude changes.

Teachers can use written test procedures utilizing true-false, multiple-choice, fill-in-the-blank, matching, or essay questions. Oral discussion, dramatizations, role-playing experiences, sociodramas, and demonstrations can also be used.

Audiotaped and/or videotaped responses or experiences provide options that some teachers and students find rewarding.

Students can be evaluated while performing psychomotor skills, i.e., the effectiveness of a film on proper golf-swing, by watching the students perform. This same performance could be videotaped for later evaluation by both the teacher and the students.

Teachers find that they can be more objective in their total evaluation of the effectiveness of the film lesson to achieve desired objectives if they also conduct a self-evaluation, considering such elements as the following:

1. WAS THE PHYSICAL CLIMATE FAVORABLE? DID I ACCOUNT FOR:
   ..... Adequate darkening in the projection screen area?
   ..... Adequate lighting for class note-taking or presentation of supplementary materials?
   ..... Suitable ventilation?
   ..... Furniture arrangements designed to give maximum advantage to viewing and listening?

2. WAS THE SCREEN:
   ..... Positioned in the correct place for viewing?
   ..... Surface the best one for the environment?
   ..... Size adequate for the room dimensions?
   ..... Adjusted for the correct height and wide enough to accommodate an unobstructed projected beam of light?

3. WAS THE PROJECTOR:
   ..... Properly set up, with the loudspeaker in an appropriate place and on a cart or table that was high enough to project an unobstructed beam of light to the screen?
   ..... Cleaned—film gate area, sprocket wheels, sound area, and guide rollers?
   ..... Sound system checked for proper operation?

..... Properly positioned to fit on and fill the screen surface?

..... Correctly threaded and ready to run before the class period began?

4. DID I USE THE "PREPARE STUDENTS" PERIOD TO:

..... Discuss the objectives of the lesson with my students?

..... Present vocabulary words and review the materials necessary to understand important elements of the film lesson?

..... Develop student interest in the film lesson?

..... Give the students specific points for which to look and listen?

..... Provide students an overview of follow-up activities and method(s) of evaluation?

5. DURING THE FILM PRESENTATION, DID I:

..... Start the film without showing the synchronizing (8-7-6-5-4-3-2-1) frames, white leader, and other non-subject content to the students?

..... Bring up the sound smoothly and at the appropriate time?

..... Set a good example by taking an active interest in the lesson?

..... Observe students, keeping alert to reactions indicating a need to reemphasize points made in the film?

..... Keep a watchful eye on the projector to be sure that no damage was done to the film?

..... Conclude the film by turning off the projection lamp and turning the sound down at the appropriate time?

Note: On the projectionist sequences listed above, if the teacher did not act as projectionist, was the student projectionist instructed in these proper operations?

6. DURING THE FOLLOW-UP, DID I:

..... Establish continuity with the film presentation by beginning my discussion and follow-up activities as soon after it as possible?

..... Give students an opportunity to discuss points of interest and ask questions?

..... Encourage and provide opportunities to engage in independent activities related to the film lesson?

..... Encourage and provide opportunities to engage in group activities, if appropriate, related to the film lesson?

..... Make assignments involving different kinds of study skills?

:..... Conduct student evaluation to see if lesson objectives were achieved?

These self-evaluation items could also be used in *teacher preparation* to serve as a checklist one might utilize to be certain that all necessary elements of the lesson planning, presentation, and follow-up are observed.

5.

Care and Storage of Films

Films should be stored in a cool place, ideally 50° F. Temperatures above 75° F. are very damaging to films, causing them to become brittle because of loss of moisture in the film base. Relative humidity should be at 50 percent. Humidity that falls below 35 percent and rises above 60 percent is also damaging to film, causing emulsion deterioration, brittleness and curling, loss of picture brilliance, and actual film shrinkage.

Films should be stored in metal or plastic cans or fiber boxes to protect them from dust and dirt. Any dirt or dust on the film will accumulate in the film gate area of the projector and cause damaging and visible scratches to appear. Storage containers will also protect films from excessive moisture. Water and film do not mix. Excessive moisture will cause the emulsion to actually slip from the film base. The moisture breaks down the binder, and the film will loose the entire emulsion layer. Figure 11 shows three types of film storage containers.

Always store film in an up-right position (see Figure 12); never stack one film on top of another for a length of time exceeding 24 hours. This excessive pressure on the edges causes warping and molecular damage.

Film should not be handled with the fingers on the picture or sound track area. Oil and moisture on the skin of the human body will cause damage. The moisture could cause

Figure 11

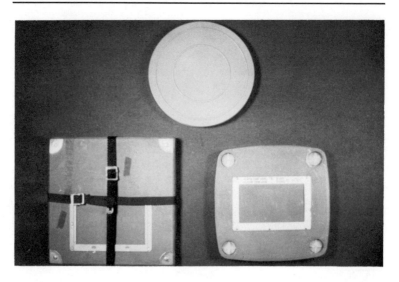

Metal or plastic containers and fiber boxes used to protect 16mm films from dust, dirt, and excessive moisture.

emulsion slippage, and the oil attracts dust and dirt to the film. Most films have at least ten or more feet of leader material on the head and tail. In projecting the film, the projectionist could handle this footage; however, when the title and picture portion are in position for projection, the projectionist should be careful to handle these content frames only along the edge and not get fingerprints on the actual film surface. A hair, tiny bits of emulsion, fingerprints, dust particles, etc., can be enlarged as much as five thousand times when projected onto the classroom screen. None of these items will enhance the film presentation or increase learning for the students. These distractions actually cause loss of viewer attention and concentration, resulting in poor assimilation and retention of film content.

Figure 12

Sixteen millimeter film storage racks. Photo courtesy of the Educational Media Center, University of Utah.

Broken films can be repaired using a film splicer and film cement or by using a mylar splicing tab. Small, inexpensive, easy-to-use splicing machines are available at all photographic supply stores. (See Appendix A for a step-by-step description of how to splice film using mylar splicing tabs.)

6.

Case Studies

Situation. A classroom teacher has ordered a film from a rental library. The film has arrived, and the teacher has previewed the film, prepared an outline, and secured some supplementary materials. He or she eagerly awaits the appointed hour to use the film. The time arrives. The eager teacher begins the introduction to a loud chorus of students, saying, "We saw that film last year—do we have to see it again?"

One possible solution. Don't fear past film experiences students have had; build upon them. Take advantage of previous experiences with the film. No student can remember all the pertinent concepts in a film. Reply to the chorus, "Really—that's fine! Tell us some of the important ideas in the film." List these items on the chalkboard or on an overhead transparency for all to see. Then go ahead and introduce the film and set up the objectives as outlined.

Situation. A teacher has shown a ten-minute how-to-do-it film on a technique involving the mounting of a chart on a piece of muslin. The teacher has given the class members a hand-out describing the steps illustrated in the film. After the film presentation, individual members of the class are encouraged to go to the school Media Center and mount a chart. Three students express interest in the project.

After several minutes have passed, a call comes from the

Media Center indicating that the Supervisor is not there and the three students do not clearly understand the mounting procedure. The teacher is busy with the 27 students who remained in the classroom to assist with other projects. What would you do with the three students in the Media Center and the 27 students in the classroom?

One possible solution. Invite the three students to come back to the room. Have them rewind the film and take it to one corner of the room and project it again on a piece of card-stock. During the projection of the film this second time, encourage them to stop the film where necessary, study the hand-out, and discuss the various steps together until they are sure they understand them. When they have finished this second viewing and feel they have a good understanding of the process, send them back to the Media Center to mount the chart. If time does not permit the actual mounting during the period, send them back tomorrow. If they need another review tomorrow, let them see the film a third time.

The 27 students in the classroom can still have the full attention of the teacher, and the film viewing should be sufficient to prepare the three students for the mounting experience in the Media Center.

Situation. A teacher has prepared a film to be used in his or her fourth period history class. The class is a 45-minute period. The film is exactly 15 minutes in length, which gives the teacher approximately 15 minutes for the introduction and 15 minutes for the follow-up review and activities. The teacher is concerned about the limited time available for introduction and follow-up activities, so he or she has set up the equipment and checked the film before the class starts to be sure that the showing of the film does not take more than 15 minutes.

The introduction is made exactly within the time limit, the film is started, and all goes well for ten minutes. Suddenly, the film breaks—the break occurring as the film is leaving the last sprocket wheel. What would you do to salvage the showing and still stay within the time limit?

One possible solution. Let the film continue to run until about five feet of film have come through the projector. This will give you enough footage to make a reel splice. Stop the machine for a few moments, make the reel splice, and then start the machine again. The lights need not be turned on. The whole reel splice operation should take no more than one minute to complete, assuming that the teacher has practiced film splicing previously—something which is highly recommended.

Situation. A high school principal has purchased a special ten-minute film that all the faculty members in the English department desire to have available, right in the school, for use whenever needed. The faculty members do not want to schedule the film on a first-available-date basis from the district media center, nor do they want to rely on a rental agency for access to the film. The content of the film is so important and vital to the English curriculum that the film can be utilized several times with the same class. For these reasons, the film has been purchased and will be kept in the English department. Upon showing the film for about the third time, the first 25 feet of the film are damaged beyond repair. The damaged footage can be removed, but the introduction and an important concept will be lost. What should be done QUICKLY to make this film available again for classes?

One possible solution. IMMEDIATELY make a phone call to the distributor of the film and order replacement footage for the film. All film producers supply replacement footage that can be spliced into the film to replace any damaged portion. With a little care, most classroom teachers can splice the replacement footage into the film, thereby making it as "good-as-new." If the urgency of the situation is explained to the film distributor, the replacement footage could be shipped within 24 hours of the request. The film could be back in service within a week's time.

Situation. A teacher in a small rural high school wishes to upgrade skills in the classroom utilization of films, filmstrips, still pictures, tapes, records, overhead transparencies, and other instructional materials. The teacher has purchased several textbooks to study, but finds that she needs some specialized guidance in her quest for these desired skills. She lives in an area where the nearest community college or university is over 100 miles away—too far to commute to attend on-campus classes. There is no media specialist or other person in the district qualified to provide effective inservice classes in instructional media utilization principles. What should be done to upgrade her skills?

One possible solution. An excellent way to upgrade competence might be through an independent study/correspondence course. Many colleges and universities in the United States offer outstanding correspondence courses in most curricular areas of media and library science. The programs provide an alternative to on-campus study and offer high quality, independent, at-home instruction, designed to guide the learner, step-by-step, through media utilization procedures and many other media and library science courses.

Situation. A high school teacher has been asked by the principal to act as the head of a "previewing" committee whose task is to arrange for, secure, and evaluate preview prints of new films in the areas of science and English. The teacher has had experience in securing the preview prints, but he is a bit unsure as to what precautions he should take to ensure that the films are not damaged during the projection of the films in the preview sessions. What should he do to be sure that he does not damage the new preview prints during the evaluation sessions?

One possible solution. Be sure the film gate area, sprocket wheels, guide rollers, and sound drum area of the projector are clean and properly adjusted. Be certain the take-up reel is of the proper size and is not bent or damaged in any way. When threading the projector, be very certain the film is threaded properly, especially in the film gate area and over the sprocket wheels. During projection of the film, stay near the projector to listen and watch for any trouble that might develop. You can tell by a change in the mechanical sound the projector emits if a malfunction has occurred. One excellent method used to check for sprocket damage is to gently feel the sprocket edge of the film just as it leaves the projector and is going onto the take-up reel. If you feel any protrusions or rough edges, immediately stop the projector and locate the source of the sprocket hole damage. This checking for proper "tracking" should be done after every 40 or 50 seconds of projection time and whenever a change is heard in the mechanical sound emitted by the motion picture projector.

7.

Future Trends

Motion pictures have a place of their own in instruction. District media centers, departments of audiovisual instruction, and centers of instructional media are no longer faced with the problem of trying to entice teachers to use motion picture films, but with supplying teacher demand for motion pictures in various formats and assisting in the selection and utilization.

The acceptance of motion picture films by teachers is partly a consequence of stylistic and technological changes in form and techniques; partly due to a revival of interest in films of the past, generated by a need for permanence and for roots in historical continuity; and partly as an aspect of the search for social understanding, self-actualization, and creative expression. This acceptance of motion picture films is firmly established, and all indications point to a continued acceptance through the decade of the 80's and perhaps the 90's.

It is anticipated, however, that in coming years many motion pictures will be "projected" in the classroom via videodiscs and videotape cassettes. Tape or disc versions of a film are much less expensive than the original 16mm film, although they have the disadvantage of not being suited to large-group showings (while being very suitable indeed for small-group or individual usage). Thus, these new media formats will not only reduce the price for the purchase of motion pictures, but also will assist in making it possible to individualize instruction utilizing motion pictures where needed.

The *initial production* of *motion* instructional materials, no matter how finally disseminated to the public, is predominantly accomplished by utilizing motion picture film. Even though color television cameras are becoming more widely available and less costly, the motion picture film camera and the sound editing machine are still the most economical and readily available methods of producing motion pictures. This situation will likely remain so well into the decade of the 80's and early 90's, even though the presentation vehicle is likely to switch from 16mm projectors to videocassette and videodisc machines.

As the new emerging media formats become widely available and accepted by educators throughout the world, motion pictures will continue to play a vital role in the educational process. Sixteen millimeter films will maintain the respected place they presently hold, especially in *large-group* instruction, well into the decade of the 80's and early 90's. Sixteen millimeter films modified and available in many alternative formats will be in demand beyond the decade of the 90's. As videodiscs and formats even more exotic and functional become available, the combining of audio with motion pictures will play an expanded role in the education of students.

The school of the future, *1990,* is expected to differ in many respects from schools as we know them today. Conceivably, in such a school:

- Instructional systems will be programmed and validated to achieve predictable results, with students under appropriate conditions and in predictable periods of time.
- Students will progress at their own individual rates,

finishing their assignments according to their ability and moving ahead as fast as they are capable of progressing.

- There will be no classrooms with fixed walls. Instead, the heart of the school will be the INSTRUCTIONAL MATERIALS CENTER, with study areas containing videodisc players, minicomputers and monitors, small viewing areas, and one or two large-group meeting spaces needed to present an occasional large-group meeting at which mediated programs or 16mm film programs of overview information and assignment directions will be given.

- There will be less attention directed to "remembering" and more to "discovery." Students will have access to an almost unlimited number of learning resources. Working in individual study stations or carrels, students will be able to view motion and still pictures through various media including videodisc, sound Super 8mm films, computer and video monitors, and as yet undeveloped formats.

Some technological innovations that will, most likely, be common in the 1990's and will have a profound impact on the quality, quantity, and methodology of instruction in American public schools, colleges, and universities are:

1. Sophisticated architectural designs for physical facilities that are planned to conserve energy, provide more space for less cost, and incorporate flexibility for future remodeling and renovation; i.e., geodesic domes, stressed shells, pressurized skins, pre-cast structures, and esoteric materials.

2. Extensive and intensive centralization of library materials. Large "systems" of computerized library and media networks will be common, with a student able to go to a computer terminal at a school or

from a centralized computer, which stores and accesses millions of pages of information.

3. Three-dimensional photography, illustrations, motion pictures, and television. Motion pictures, utilizing holographic photography, will bring realism to the classroom or the private home that will provide opportunities for learners to sense they are actually an integral part of the occurrence, environment, or situation.

4. Simple and inexpensive recording and playback equipment for use in the home that utilizes magnetic tapes, discs, fiber optics, and lasers. Students will be able to check-out from the Media Center or other central storage facility all kinds of visual and audio materials to assist in the learning process—utilized in the home on their own projection and listening devices for independent or small-group study. These devices and services will also provide new techniques and institutions for *adult education*.

5. Instant motion picture film. Students and teachers will be able to produce instant motion segments of events, occurrences, and happenings for small-group and independent study. These low-cost motion pictures will bring the world into the home and classroom. Linked to satellite communication networks and computer terminals, students will be able to secure motion pictures for study in learning centers or in the privacy of the home.

8.

Suggested Student Projects

1. Have a student or student committee select a sound film and "preview" it. Instruct the student(s) to complete the following evaluation form. As an outcome of this previewing, have the student(s) introduce and show the film to the class. Include in this exercise the preparation and administration of a pretest and posttest evaluation. (Elementary, Jr. High, Sr. High.)

Title: ....

Producer: ....

Sound: ...... Silent: ...... Color: ...... B&W: ...... Reels: ......

Actual running time: ...... Production date: ...... Most

Appropriate Grade Level: ....

1. Short description of content:

2. How might the film be used?

3. List any outstanding strengths or weaknesses:

4. List vocabulary words:

2. Train a student to be a projectionist. Include in the training proper room environment and set-up, proper care and operation of the projector, and correct handling of the film. Arrange to have this student show films to your class and other classes in the building. (Elementary.)

3. Have a student design a STUDENT PROJECTIONIST CARD, which indicates that a student has been trained in the proper set-up of the environment, correct operation of a 16mm projector, and how to properly care for film. This card will be presented to all students trained as student projectionists. (Elementary.)

4. Have a student design a CERTIFICATE OF ACHIEVE-MENT, which indicates that a student has completed training as a certified projectionist, competent in proper classroom environment set-up, correct operation of a 16mm projector, and proper handling and care of motion picture film. This certificate will be presented to all students trained as projectionists. (Elementary.)

5. Assign a student committee the responsibility of previewing the next film to be used in class. As an outcome of this preview, have them prepare a classroom bulletin board designed to assist in the introduction of the up-coming film lesson. (Elementary, Jr. High, Sr. High.)

6. Have a student write a brief description to present to the entire class of the following cinematic camera techniques: microphotography, slow-motion photography, time-lapse photography, animation, macrophotography, X-ray photography, and telescope/space photography. The student could also go to the district film library and select films that would illustrate each technique. A short clip of each technique could be shown to the class. (Jr. High, Sr. High.)

7. Assign a student committee the responsibility for writing the script for production of a sound Super 8mm film. After the script has been written and critiqued, prepare a story-board outline of the various scenes to be photographed. (Jr. High, Sr. High.)

8. After the story-board outline has been completed, assign students to various tasks needed to *SHOOT* the sound film. The committees or groups needed to complete the film are: photographers (camerapersons), actors, directors, credits and cue graphic artists, set, props, and costume technicians, and sound technicians. You will *only* need a good quality sound camera, a tripod, two or more flood lights for indoor photography, and a boom stand for the microphone. If you do all the photography outdoors utilizing "natural" lighting, the flood lights will not be needed. (Jr. High, Sr. High.)

9. After the film has been photographed, assign two or three students the task of editing the film in preparation for screening before the class or entire school. A viewer and splicer will be needed. (Jr. High, Sr. High.)

10. Arrange for the film to be presented to the P.T.A., a local civic club, another school, etc. Have a student committee be responsible for the presentation of the film and the details involved in the selection of the theme, writing, shooting, and editing phases needed to complete the production. (Jr. High, Sr. High.)

11. Students can be assigned the various tasks, as outlined in activities #7, #8, and #9, to prepare and shoot a "documentary" film of some real-life situations or people in the local community. This film could be shown to various groups as outlined in activity #10 plus as a *special* presentation over a local television station as a community "human-interest" story. (Jr. High, Sr. High.)

12. Secure some clear 16mm film stock, a set of water-based nylon pens, and a good quality cassette tape recorder. Assign a student committee to select an appropriate piece of music and have them draw designs, lines, shapes, etc., on the clear film stock to accompany the music, thereby creating a visual impression of the music. (Jr. High, Sr. High.)

13. The narration on some films, due to datedness, inaccuracies, omissions, etc., may be inappropriate for use in

a particular class. Assign a student or student committee to rewrite the narration. The new script can either be presented orally while showing the film or recorded on a cassette tape and synchronized to the moving pictures. (Elementary, Jr. High, Sr. High.)

14. Some 16mm films, such as "Boogie Doodle," "Fiddle De Dee," "Boarded Window," "Blades and Brass," "Flight," etc., are produced without narration. Assign a student or student committee to write an appropriate script to accompany the pictorial portion of one of these films. (Elementary, Jr. High, Sr. High.)

15. Many films utilize an "open-end" technique in the presentation of information, a technique which presents a problem but which does not attempt to provide its solution. After showing such a film in class, divide the class into small groups and have each group discuss how it would solve the problem. Have the groups report their solution either as an oral or written report. As a whole group, analyze the results of each group's contribution. (Elementary, Jr. High, Sr. High.)

16. After a film showing, divide the class into small groups and assign the groups specific topics covered in the film as areas to obtain more detailed information. This will involve additional reading in texts, encyclopedias, periodical literature, microforms, etc. Have the topics reported as written and oral supplements to the film content. (Elementary, Jr. High, Sr. High.)

17. Assign a student or committee to seek out and invite a resource person from the community to visit the classroom to enlarge and expand upon ideas presented by the film. Have the committee prepare an outline of information, desired by class members, to be discussed by the community resource person. (Elementary, Jr. High, Sr. High.)

9.

Glossary of Terms

Ambient light: the uncontrolled light entering the viewing area when projecting a film or other projected materials.

Animation: a photographic technique which takes one picture at a time of· a series of drawings depicting movement.

Aperture: an opening in the 16mm projector or other projection device through which light passes to accomplish the projection of one frame of film.

Base: the shiny side of 16mm film which is composed of cellulose-acetate plastic and comprises the bulk of the thickness.

Beaded screen: a reflective surface composed of glass beads adhered to a white fabric.

Behavioral objective: behavior the learner is able to demonstrate at the time the teaching/learning process is concluded, described in terms which permit the learner to know what he or she should be capable of doing and on what basis evaluation is to occur, whether it be mastery of information, performance of skills, or inventive and creative endeavors.

Binder: thin layer of glue used to hold the emulsion to the base in a 16mm film.

Direct—real-life: films which use the camera and microphone to record and present events precisely as they occur, with little or no editing.

Documentary: films specializing in the realistic and factual treatment of a subject without the benefit of professional actors and contrived stage settings.

Drama—fictional: films which present believable expositions of literary works.

Drama—true-life: films which depict events in the lives of real people.

Educational collaborator: a subject-matter specialist who acts as an advisor in educational materials production to insure the accuracy of the instructional content.

Emulsion: a gelatine substance in which the picture image of a 16mm film is formed. The emulsion side is the dull, less shiny side of the film.

Film gate area/channel: area in a 16mm projector where the film is clamped or locked to facilitate projection of one frame of film. The film gate is composed of two parts—pressure plate and aperture opening. The pressure plate fits into the film channel. The aperture opening is in the lateral center of the film gate area.

Fluoroscope: a machine for examining internal structures by viewing the shadows cast on a fluorescent screen by objects or parts through which X-rays are directed. The shadows vary in intensity according to the density of the object or parts.

Frame: one picture area on a 16mm film, filmstrip, or slide.

Guide rollers: device used to guide the 16mm film into the proper channel/path as it passes through the projector during the projection of the film.

Intermittent device: a mechanism located in the film gate area of a 16mm projector which accomplishes the movement of one frame of film in front of the aperture opening for projection. Sometimes called the "intermittent claw."

Keystoning: an out-of-square image on a projection screen, resulting when the plane of the screen and the plane of the projected material are not parallel to each other.

Lenticular screen: a reflective surface composed of a silver, corrugated, metallic material.

Light valve: a device utilizing either metallic ribbons set in a magnetic field or a galvanometer (an instrument used to measure electric current) to produce the optical sound track of a 16mm film.

Macrophotography: a technique that utilizes a close-up lens on a motion picture camera to enlarge small objects or creatures such as an ant, bee, or brine fly—generally used to photograph the "small world" of nature.

Matte screen: a reflective surface composed of a flat, white fabric.

Microphotography: a photographic technique requiring a special camera attached to a microscope with a lighting apparatus that provides enough light to record microscopic images on film.

Persistence of vision: the ability of the retina of the human eye to retain an image for a short time after the stimulus for the image has disappeared.

Reel splice: method employed to make a *speedy* joining of a broken 16mm film during projection by overlapping the two separated sections, winding them a few turns on the take-up reel, and continuing with the film screening.

Religious films: those films which emphasize religious history or events and dramatize occurrences involving moral and spiritual values.

Slow-motion photography: a technique utilizing a special motion picture camera which takes more frames per second than the sound motion picture plays back.

Splicing tabs: mylar (sticky-backed, perforated along one edge, 16mm wide) strips of plastic used to join two pieces of a broken film.

Sponsored films: motion picture films produced by business and industrial firms for the purpose of informing the viewer about the company and its many products.

Sprocket holes: perforations along the edge of the film.

Sprocket wheel: device of a 16mm projector which turns to drive the film through the projector. Has teeth on one edge that engage with the sprocket holes in the film thereby providing positive movement during projection.

Stop-on-frame: device on a 16mm projector which permits one frame of the film to be projected for an indefinite period of time without doing physical damage to the film (the projected image will be dimmed slightly by the heat absorbing screen designed to prevent any physical damage).

Superimposed: words or phrases that are layed on top of the picture portion of a frame of film and then re-photographed to give a composite of pictorial content and the words or phrases.

Synopsis: a statement giving a brief, general overview of the film content.

Telelecture: an interview technique utilizing the telephone, long-distance dialing, and an amplification system that allow a guest speaker to address and interact with distant students.

Telescope/space photography: technique which utilizes a telescope or a telescopic lens to photograph distant objects.

Tension rollers: device used to hold the film tightly around the sound drum in a 16mm projector.

Thaumathrope: device composed of a still disc-shaped paper attached to a round stick with a bird painted on one side and a bird cage on the other and used to illustrate *persistence of vision.*

Time-lapse photography: a technique which utilizes a special motion picture camera and an intricate lighting arrangement to take single pictures at regular intervals over an extended period of time.

Travelogue: films which present geographical information

about towns, cities, counties, states, nations, regions, continents, rivers, lakes, oceans, etc.

X-ray photography: a photographic process that utilizes the fluoroscope screen of an X-ray machine.

10.

Hardware Producers — 16mm Projectors

AIC PHOTO, INC.
168 Glen Cove Road
Carle Place, New York 11514

A.V.E. CORPORATION
250 West 54th Street
New York, New York 10019

BELL AND HOWELL COMPANY
Audio Visual Products Division
7100 McCormick Road
Chicago, Illinois 60645

BERGEN EXPO SYSTEMS, INC.
1088 Main Avenue
Clifton, New Jersey 07011

BUSCH FILM & EQUIPMENT COMPANY
214 South Hamilton Street
Saginaw, Michigan 48602

EASTMAN KODAK COMPANY
343 State Street
Rochester, New York 14650

EIKI INTERNATIONAL, INC.
27882 Camino Capistrano
Laguna Niguel, California 92677

ELMO MFG. CORPORATION
32-10 57th Street
Woodside, New York 11377

KALART VICTOR CORPORATION
P.O. Box 112
Hultenius Street
Plainville, Connecticut 06062

OPTICAL RADIATION CORPORATION
6352 North Irwindale Avenue
Azusa, California 91702

PAILLARD, INC.
1900 Lower Road
Linden, New Jersey 07036

SINGER EDUCATION SYSTEMS
3750 Monroe Avenue
Rochester, New York 14603

TRIANGLE PROJECTORS, INC.
P.O. Box 30039
Chicago, Illinois 60630

VIEWLEX AUDIO VISUAL, INC.
1 Broadway Avenue
Holbrook, Long Island
New York 11741

11.

Software Producers — 16mm Films

ACADEMY FILMS DISTRIBUTION COMPANY
P.O. Box 3414
Orange, California 92665

ACI FILMS, INC.
35 West 45th Street
New York, New York 10036

AIMS INSTRUCTIONAL MEDIA SERVICES, INC.
P.O. Box 1010
Hollywood, California 90038

ALEMAN FILMS
P.O. Box 76244
Los Angeles, California 90005

AMERICAN DOCUMENTARY FILMS
336 West 84th Street
New York, New York 10024

AMERICAN EDUCATIONAL FILMS
331 North Maple Drive
Beverly Hills, California 90210

AMERICAN LEGION
Motion Picture Section
P.O. Box 1055
Indianapolis, Indiana 46206

ASPECT IV EDUCATIONAL FILMS
21 Charles Street
Westport, Connecticut 06880

ASSOCIATED FILMS CONSULTANTS, INC.
501 Madison Avenue
New York, New York 10022

ASSOCIATION/STERLING EDUCATIONAL FILMS
241 East 34th Street
New York, New York 10016

ATLANTIS PRODUCTIONS, INC.
1252 La Granda Drive
Thousand Oaks, California 91360

AUDICATION, INC.
18 La Salle Street
Elsah, Illinois 62028

AUDIO PRODUCTIONS/EDUCATIONAL SERVICES
630 Ninth Avenue
New York, New York 10036

A-V EXPLORATIONS, INC.
505 Delaware Avenue
Buffalo, New York 14202

ARTHUR BARR PRODUCTIONS, INC.
P.O. Box 7-C
Pasadena, California 91104

BENCHMARK FILMS, INC.
145 Scarborough Road
Briarcliff Manor, New York 10510

BFA EDUCATIONAL MEDIA
2211 Michigan Avenue
Santa Monica, California 90404

BILLY BUDD FILMS, INC.
235 East 57th Street
New York, New York 10022

ANTI-DEFAMATION LEAGUE OF B'NAI B'RITH
315 Lexington Avenue
New York, New York 10016

STEPHEN BOSUSTOW PRODUCTIONS
20548 Pacific Coast Highway
Malibu, California 90265

ROBERT J. BRADY COMPANY
130 Q Street, NE
Washington, D.C. 20002

BRIGHAM YOUNG UNIVERSITY
Department of Motion Picture Production
Provo, Utah 84601

E.C. BROWN TRUST FOUNDATION
Mrs. Ruth R. Wolfe, Executive Secretary
3170 South West 87th Avenue
P.O. Box 25130
Portland, Oregon 97225

CAMPBELL FILMS
Saxtons River, Vermont 05154

CAMPUS FILM DISTRIBUTORS CORPORATION
20 East 46th Street
New York, New York 10017

CAROUSEL FILMS, INC.
1501 Broadway
New York, New York 10036

CAVALCADE PRODUCTIONS, INC.
P.O. Box 801
Wheaton, Illinois 60187

CCM FILMS, INC.
866 Third Avenue
New York, New York 10021

CENTRON EDUCATIONAL FILMS
1621 West Ninth Street
Lawrence, Kansas 66044

CHURCHILL FILMS
662 North Robertson Boulevard
Los Angeles, California 90069

COLONIAL WILLIAMSBURG FOUNDATION
P.O. Box C
Williamsburg, Virginia 23185

COLUMBIA UNIVERSITY PRESS
562 West 113th Street
New York, New York 10025

COMMUNICATIONS GROUP WEST
6430 Sunset Boulevard
Hollywood, California 90028

CONCORDIA FILMS
3558 South Jefferson
St. Louis, Missouri 63118

CONNECTICUT FILMS, INC.
6 Cobble Hill Road
Westport, Connecticut 06880

CONTEMPORARY/MCGRAW-HILL FILMS
330 West 42nd Street
New York, New York 10036

CORONET FILMS
Coronet Building
65 East South Water Street
Chicago, Illinois 60601

CREATIVE FILM SOCIETY
14558 Valerio Street
Van Nuys, California 91405

CREATIVISION, INC.
295 West 4th Street
New York, New York 10014

DAVIDSON FILMS
3701 Buchanan Street
San Francisco, California 94123

DIBIE-DASH PRODUCTIONS, INC.
Motion Pictures
4949 Hollywood Boulevard (Suite 208)
Hollywood, California 90027

DISCOVERY TEACHING FILMS, INC.
P.O. Box 424
Carmel Valley, California 93924

DOUBLEDAY MULTIMEDIA
1371 Reynolds Avenue
Santa Ana, California 92705

EDUCATIONAL FILM DISTRIBUTORS, LTD.
191 Eglinton Avenue East
Toronto 315, Ontario, Canada

EDUCATIONAL MEDIA
211 East 43rd Street
New York, New York 10036

EDUCATIONAL MEDIA DISTRIBUTION CENTER
Conference of Executives of American Schools for
  the Deaf, Inc.
5034 Wisconsin Avenue, NW
Washington, D.C. 20016

ENCYCLOPAEDIA BRITANNICA
425 North Michigan Avenue
Chicago, Illinois 60611

FAMILY FILMS
5823 Santa Monica Boulevard
Hollywood, California 90038

FARM FILM FOUNDATION
Suite 424, Southern Building
Washington, D.C. 20005

FILM ORIGINALS
6536 Robertson Drive
Boise, Idaho 83705

FILMFAIR COMMUNICATIONS
Distributed by Trend Films Corporation
P.O. Box 69680
Los Angeles, California 90069

FILMS, INCORPORATED
1144 Wilmette Avenue
Wilmette, Illinois 60091

FIREBIRD FILMS
203 Glen Avenue
Sea Cliff, Long Island
New York 11579

FOLKLORE PUPPETS
657 Avenue C
Bayonne, New Jersey 07002

GENERAL ELECTRIC EDUCATIONAL FILMS
60 Washington Avenue
Schenectady, New York 12305

GIRL SCOUTS OF THE USA
830 Third Avenue
New York, New York 10022

THE GRAPHIC CURRICULUM
P.O. Box 565
Lenox Hill Station
New York, New York 10021

GROVE PRESS, INC.
53 East 11th Street
New York, New York 10003

GROVER FILMS
P.O. Box 303
Monterey, California 93940

GUIDANCE INFORMATION CENTER
Academy Avenue
Saxtons River, Vermont 05154

HANDEL FILM CORPORATION
8730 Sunset Boulevard
West Hollywood, California 90069

HARRIS-TUCHMAN PRODUCTIONS, INC.
751 North Highland Avenue
Hollywood, California 90038

HARTLEY PRODUCTIONS
Cat Rock Road
Cos Cob, Connecticut 06807

HARVEST A-V, INC.
309 Fifth Avenue
New York, New York 10016

ALFRED HIGGINS PRODUCTIONS
9100 Sunset Boulevard
Los Angeles, California 90069

HOLT, RINEHART, AND WINSTON, INC.
383 Madison Avenue
New York, New York 10017

IMPERIAL CHEMICAL INDUSTRIES (NEW YORK), INC.
P.O. Box 1274
151 South Street
Stamford, Connecticut 06904

INDIANA UNIVERSITY AUDIO-VISUAL CENTER
Bloomington, Indiana 47401

INTERFILM
Cinema East
Drawer 13955K
Atlanta, Georgia 30324

INTERNATIONAL FILM BUREAU, INC.
332 South Michigan Avenue
Chicago, Illinois 60604

IOWA STATE UNIVERSITY FILM PRODUCTION UNIT
Alice Norton House
Iowa State University of Science and Technology
Ames, Iowa 50010

JOURNAL FILMS, INC.
909 West Diversey Parkway
Chicago, Illinois 60614

KAYFETZ-EDUTEC PRODUCTIONS
295 West 4th Street
New York, New York 10014

STACY KEACH PRODUCTIONS
12240 Ventura Boulevard
Studio City, California 91604

WALTER J. KLEIN COMPANY, LTD.
6301 Carmel Road
Charlotte, North Carolina 28211

LEARNING CORPORATION OF AMERICA
711 Fifth Avenue
New York, New York 10022

LEXINGTON SCHOOL FOR THE DEAF
26-26 75th Street
Jackson Heights, Queens
New York 11370

LUTHERAN FILM LIBRARY
267 West 25th Street
New York, New York 10001

HAROLD MANTELL, INC.
P.O. Box 378
Princeton, New Jersey 08540

MASS MEDIA ASSOCIATES
1720 Chouteau Avenue
St. Louis, Missouri 63103

MCGRAW-HILL BOOK COMPANY
330 West 42nd Street
New York, New York 10036

THE METROPOLITAN OPERA GUILD, INC.
1865 Broadway
New York, New York 10023

MILADY VISUAL AIDS PUBLISHING CORPORATION
3839 White Plains Road
Bronx, New York 10467

MODERN LEARNING AIDS
P.O. Box 302
Rochester, New York 14603

MODERN TALKING PICTURE SERVICE
2323 New Hyde Park Road
Long Island, New York 11040

ARTHUR MOKIN PRODUCTIONS, INC.
17 West 60th Street
New York, New York 10023

MORELAND-LATCHFORD PRODUCTIONS, LTD.
Sales Department
43 Dundas Street West
Toronto 102, Ontario, Canada

THE MOVIE HOUSE
P.O. Box 3241
Stanford, California 94305

NATIONAL AUDIOVISUAL CENTER
National Archives and Records Service
United States General Services Administration
Washington, D.C. 20409

NATIONAL COAL ASSOCIATION
Education Division
Coal Building
1130 17th Street, NW
Washington, D.C. 20036

NATIONAL COUNCIL OF CHURCHES
Broadcasting and Film Commission
475 Riverside Drive—Room 860
New York, New York 10027

NATIONAL EDUCATIONAL MEDIA, INC.
3518 West Cahuenga Boulevard
Hollywood, California 90068

NBC EDUCATIONAL ENTERPRISES
30 Rockefeller Plaza
New York, New York 10020

NEW YORK UNIVERSITY FILM LIBRARY
41 Press Annex
Washington Square
New York, New York 10003

NORTHERN FILMS
P.O. Box 98—Main Office Station
Seattle, Washington 98111

NORTHWESTERN UNIVERSITY PRESS
1735 Benson Avenue
Evanston, Illinois 60201

OFFICIAL INDUSTRIES, INC.
776 Grand Avenue
Ridgefield, New Jersey 07657

OHIO STATE UNIVERSITY
Film Distribution Supervisor
Department of Photography and Cinema
156 West 19th Avenue
Columbus, Ohio 43210

PAN-AMERICAN DEVELOPMENT FOUNDATION
17th and Constitution Avenue, NW
Washington, D.C. 20006

PAULIST PRODUCTIONS
Insight Films
17575 Pacific Coast Highway
Pacific Palisades, California 90272

PERENNIAL EDUCATION, INC.
1825 Willow Road
Northfield, Illinois 60093

PETITE FILM COMPANY
708 North 62nd Street
Seattle, Washington 98103

PHOTOLAB, INC.
25 Georgia Avenue, NW
Washington, D.C. 20011

PLANNED PARENTHOOD—WORLD POPULATION
810 7th Avenue
New York, New York 10019

PROFESSIONAL ARTS, INC.
P.O. Box 8484
Universal City, California 91608

PSYCHOLOGICAL FILMS
205 West Twentieth Street
Santa Ana, California 92805

REGISTRY OF MEDICAL TECHNOLOGISTS (ASCP)
P.O. Box 4872
Chicago, Illinois 60680

SANTA FE FILM BUREAU
Room 100—121 East Sixth
Los Angeles, California 90014

SCIENCE RESEARCH ASSOCIATES, INC.
568 University Avenue, Suite G
Palo Alto, California 94301

SCOTT, FORESMAN, AND COMPANY
855 California Avenue
Palo Alto, California 94304

SHELL FILM LIBRARY
450 North Meridian Street
Indianapolis, Indiana 46204

SHERBOURNE PRESS
1640 South La Clenega Boulevard
Los Angeles, California 90035

SPORTLITE FILMS
20 North Wacker Drive
Chicago, Illinois 60606

STANTON FILMS
7934 Santa Monica Boulevard
Los Angeles, California 90046

TEACHING FILM CUSTODIANS, INC.
25 West 43rd Street
New York, New York 10036

TEACHING FILMS, INC.
P.O. Box 66824
Houston, Texas 77006

TEACHING RESOURCES/MULTIMEDIA
Educational Service for *The New York Times*
509 Madison Avenue
New York, New York 10022

TEXTURE FILMS, INC.
1600 Broadway
New York, New York 10019

THORNE FILMS
Dept. Gc-71, 1229 University Avenue
Boulder, Colorado 80302

TIME-LIFE FILMS
Time & Life Building
Rockefeller Center
New York, New York 10020

UNIT PRODUCTIONS
c/o 1400 University Club Building
136 East South Temple
Salt Lake City, Utah 84111

UNITED STATES ATOMIC ENERGY COMMISSION
Washington, D.C. 20545

UNIVERSITY OF CALIFORNIA EXTENSION MEDIA
Berkeley, California 94720

THE UNIVERSITY OF IOWA AUDIOVISUAL CENTER
Iowa City, Iowa 52240

UNIVERSITY OF MINNESOTA
Department of Audio-Visual Extension
2037 University Avenue SE
Minneapolis, Minnesota 55455

VISUAL EDUCATION SERVICE
The Divinity School
Yale University
409 Prospect Street
New Haven, Connecticut 06511

VOCATIONAL FILMS
111 Euclid Avenue
Park Ridge, Illinois 60068

WARREN SCHLOAT PRODUCTIONS, INC.
Pleasantville, New York 10570

WAYNE STATE UNIVERSITY
Center for Instructional Technology
Detroit, Michigan 48202

WESTON WOODS STUDIOS
Weston, Connecticut 06880

JOHN WILEY & SONS, INC.
605 Third Avenue
New York, New York 10016

12.

Bibliography

BOOKS

Cross, A.J.F., and Irene F. Cypher. *Audio-Visual Education,* Thomas V. Crowell Company, New York, New York, 1961, pp. 45-72.

Dale, Edgar. *Audiovisual Methods in Teaching, Third Edition,* Dryden Press, New York, New York, 1969, pp. 389-428.

Davidson, Raymond L. *Audiovisual Machines,* International Textbook Company, Scranton, Pennsylvania, 1969, pp. 103-153.

DeKieffer, Robert, and Lee W. Cockran. *Manual of Audio-Visual Techniques,* Prentice-Hall, Inc., Englewood Cliffs, New Jersey, 1955, pp. 123-140.

Eboch, Sidney C., and George W. Cochran. *Operating Audio-Visual Equipment,* Chandler Publishing Company, San Francisco, California, 1968, pp. 7-28.

Erickson, Carlton W.H., and David H. Curl. *Fundamentals of Teaching with Audiovisual Technology, Second Edition,* The Macmillan Company, New York, New York, 1972, pp. 117-127.

Finn, James D. *The Audio-Visual Equipment Manual,* Dryden Press, New York, New York, 1957, pp. 1-84.

Jones, Emily S. *Manual on Film Evaluation, Revised Edition,* Educational Film Library Association, New York, New York, 1974, 30 pages.

Kinder, James S. *Using Audio-Visual Materials in Education,* American Book Company, New York, New York, 1965, pp. 50-61.

National Audio-Visual Association, Inc. *The Audio Visual Equipment Directory* (annual), Fairfax, Virginia.

Oates, Stanton C. *Self-Instructional Manual—Audiovisual Equipment,* Wm. C. Brown Company, Dubuque, Iowa, 1975, pp. 55-162.

Sands, Lester B. *Audio-Visual Procedures in Teaching,* Ronald Press Company, New York, New York, 1956, pp. 344-378.

Thomas, R. Murray, and Sherman G. Swartout. *Integrated Teaching Materials,* David McKay Company, Inc., New York, New York, 1963, pp. 137-159.

Weisgerber, Robert A., Editor. *Instructional Process and Media Innovation,* Rand McNally and Company, Chicago, Illinois, 1968, pp. 343-367 and pp. 526-544.

MEDIA

Basic Film Terms: A Visual Dictionary, 16mm film, color, 14 minutes, Pyramid Films Company, 2801 Colorado Avenue, Santa Monica, California 90404.

Bringing the World to the Classroom, 35mm single-frame filmstrip, black and white, 45 frames, Wayne State University, CIT Productions Center, 5035 Woodward, Detroit, Michigan 48202.

Children Make Movies, 16mm film, black and white, 10 minutes, McGraw-Hill Films, 1221 Avenue of the Americas, New York, New York 10020.

Facts About Film, 3rd edition, 16mm film, color, 12 minutes, International Film Bureau, Inc., 332 South Michigan Avenue, Chicago, Illinois 60604.

Facts About Projection, 3rd edition, 16mm film, color, 16 minutes, International Film Bureau, Inc., 332 South Michigan Avenue, Chicago, Illinois 60604.

A Film About Cinematography, 16mm film, color, 18 minutes, International Film Bureau, Inc., 332 South Michigan Avenue, Chicago, Illinois 60604.

A Film About Filmmaking, 16mm film, color, 17 minutes, International Film Bureau, Inc., 332 South Michigan Avenue, Chicago, Illinois 60604.

Film Research and Learning, 16mm film, black and white, 16 minutes, International Film Bureau, Inc., 332 South Michigan Avenue, Chicago, Illinois 60604.

Film Tactics, 16mm film, black and white, 22 minutes, National Audiovisual Center, National Archives & Records Service, General Service Administration, Washington, D.C. 20409.

Film and You: Using the Classroom Film, 16mm film, color, 13 minutes, Bailey-Film Associates, 2211 Michigan Avenue, Santa Monica, California 90404.

How to Splice Film, 35mm single-frame filmstrip, color, 38 frames, Bailey-Film Associates, 2211 Michigan Avenue, Santa Monica, California 90404.

How to Splice Film, 16mm film, black and white, 10 minutes, Encyclopaedia Britannica Educational Corporation, 425 North Michigan Avenue, Chicago, Illinois 60611.

How to Teach with Films, 16mm film, black and white, 16 minutes, Cathedral Film, Inc., 140 North Hollywood Way, Burbank, California 91521.

How to Use a Teaching Film, 35mm single-frame filmstrip, color, 43 frames, William H. Allen Company, 808 Lockern Street, Los Angeles, California 90049.

Instructional Films—The New Way to Greater Education, 16mm film, black and white, 27 minutes, Coronet Films, Coronet Building, 65 East South Water Street, Chicago, Illinois 60604.

Making Films That Teach, 16mm film, black and white, 20 minutes, Encyclopaedia Britannica Educational Corporation, 425 North Michigan Avenue, Chicago, Illinois 60611.

Making a Sound Film, 16mm film, color, 13 minutes, International Film Bureau, Inc., 332 South Michigan Avenue, Chicago, Illinois 60604.

Motion Picture Projector Operation Programs, slides or filmstrips, 80 frames each, captioned, color, Media Systems, Inc., 3637 East 7800 South, Salt Lake City, Utah 84121.

Show Must Go On, 16mm film, black and white, 20 minutes, Bell and Howell Corporation, Film Division, 7100 McCormick Road, Chicago, Illinois 60645.

Time-Lapse Photography, 16mm film, color, 19 minutes, International Film Bureau, Inc., 332 South Michigan Avenue, Chicago, Illinois 60604.

Understanding Movies, 16mm film, color, 13 minutes, Perspective Film, Inc., 369 West Erie Street, Chicago, Illinois 60610.

Understanding Movies, 16mm film, black and white, 17 minutes, Teaching Films Custodians, 25 West 43rd Street, New York, New York 10036.

The Unique Contribution, 16mm film, color, 33 minutes, Encyclopaedia Britannica Educational Corporation, 425 North Michigan Avenue, Chicago, Illinois 60611.

Using the Classroom Film, 16mm film, black and white, 21 minutes, Encyclopaedia Britannica Educational Corporation, 425 North Michigan Avenue, Chicago, Illinois 60611.

PERIODICALS

Baird, James F. "Criteria Used to Select 16mm Films," *Audiovisual Instruction,* Volume 20, Number 4, April, 1975, pp. 18-20.

Cramer, Hetty. "Super Cinderella—Fourth Graders Put Fantasy on Film," *Audiovisual Instruction,* Volume 21, Number 3, March, 1976, pp. 70-71.

Day, Joseph A. "The Pitfalls of Evaluating Instructional Materials," *Audiovisual Instruction,* Volume 21, Number 5, May, 1976, pp. 26-27.

Hoban, Charles F., Jr. "The State of the Art of Films in Instruction," *Audiovisual Instruction,* Volume 20, Number 4, April, 1975, pp. 30-34.

Horseman, Maurine. "Can Video Bring Happiness to a 16mm Film Production?" *Audiovisual Instruction,* Volume 21, Number 1, January, 1975, pp. 32-33.

Houser, Roland L., Eileen J. Houser, and Adrian Moudfrands. "Learning a Motion and Nonmotion Concept by Motion Picture Versus Slide Presentations," *AV Communications Review,* Volume 18, Number 4, Winter, 1970, pp. 424-430.

Locatis, Craig, and Francis D. Atkinson. "A Guide to Instructional Selection," *Educational Technology,* Volume 16, Number 8, August, 1976, pp. 19-21.

Nibeck, Richard G. "Which Medium for the Future?" *Audiovisual Instruction,* Volume 21, Number 1, January, 1976, pp. 12-13 and p. 71.

Spitzer, Dean R., and Timothy O. McNerny. "Operationally Defining Visual Literacy—A Research Challenge, " *Audiovisual Instruction,* Volume 20, Number 7, September, 1975, pp. 30-31.

Thiagarajan, Sivasailam. "Making Protocol Films: An Exercise in Concept Teaching," *Educational Technology,* Volume 15, Number 9, September, 1975, pp. 38-40.

Wools, Blanche, and David V. Loertscher. "Preview—One Step in the Selection Process," *Audiovisual Instruction,* Volume 20, Number 4, April, 1975, pp. 21-23.

Appendix A

16mm Film Splicing

Small, relatively inexpensive, easy-to-use splicing machines
are available for purchase in all photographic supply stores.
However, most school administrators do not budget the
funds or expend the effort necessary to secure a mechanical
splicer and make it available for the repair of films broken in
classroom projection. As a consequence, teachers do not have
an effective method for making an appropriate splice so that
broken films can be mended for immediate re-showing or
future use.

Some inappropriate methods for joining the ends of
broken films that teachers use are Scotch tape, masking tape,
straight pins, or even metal staples. These methods not only
do not provide an adequate splice, but also they can do
actual harm to mechanical parts of the motion picture
projector, especially to the film gate area, sprocket wheels,
sound drum, and tensioning devices.

The sticky-backed, mylar splicing tab offers an inexpensive, easy-to-use method of joining the ends of a broken film
that will provide a strong splice and will not damage
delicate parts of the motion picture projector. The sticky-
backed, mylar splicing tabs are available in all photographic
supply stores; however, the details for utilizing the tabs in
splicing motion picture films are not readily available, either
as instructions that accompany the tabs or in photographic
texts. Consequently, the detailed, illustrated process follows:

Step 1. "Butt" the two edges of the broken 16mm film together, emulsion or the duller, less shiny side, UP. As exact registration of the broken edges is critical, align the two edges together carefully. *Do not* allow any open space along the butted edges. If exact alignment is not accomplished and maintained, the mylar splicing tab will not align properly with the sprocket holes in the 16mm film. Always handle the film from the edges, along the sprocket hole and sound track areas. DO NOT touch the picture area if at all possible.

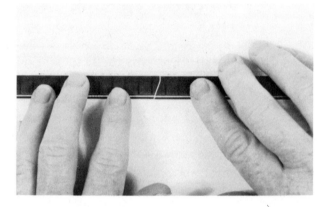

Step 2. Carefully place four small pieces of masking tape, about two inches back from the break, on each edge of the two pieces of the broken 16mm film. These four pieces of masking tape will hold the broken parts of the film in perfect alignment. Place two of the four pieces on the sprocket hole side and two on the sound track side of the film, being careful so that the tape does not extend into the picture portion of the film.

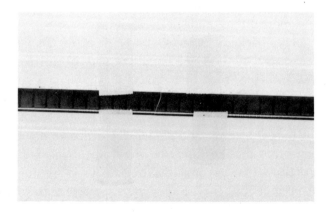

Step 3. Place the splicing tab, complete with the protective paper covering the sticky area intact, on the film. *Most* carefully align the holes in the splicing tab with the sprocket holes along the edge of the film. The tab is placed with the paper side *down* on the film—the shiny, mylar tab will be *up*. Again, be careful to properly align the holes in the tab with the sprocket holes in the film.

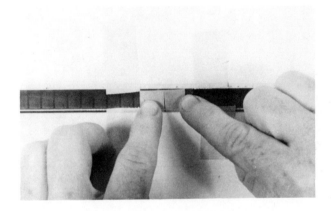

Step 4. Place one finger on the left edge/side of the splicing tab. Check alignment of the sprocket holes once again, and hold it securely against the film. Exert enough finger pressure to hold the tab securely in position. Do not let the tab slip. Remove the protective paper from the sticky portion on the right-hand side of the splicing tab. The paper removes easily, but you must be careful so that the edges of the mylar tab are not damaged as the paper is peeled away. Press down firmly on this right side of the tab to cause it to adhere to the film.

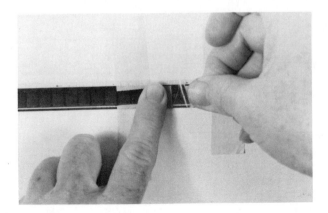

Step 5. Place a finger on the right edge (the one you just adhered down) of the splicing tab and exert enough finger pressure to hold it securely in place against the film. Slowly and *very* carefully remove the protective paper from the sticky left side of the splicing tab. After the paper is removed, press down on the tab to cause it to adhere to the film surface.

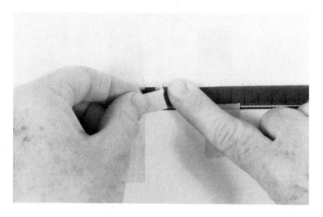

Step 6. Using a smooth, hard, rounded instrument like the end of a ball point pen, burnish or rub over the entire surface of the splicing tab, thereby assuring a good, complete contact of the tab with the film. Any area of the tab that is not completely adhered will have a "milky" or frosted appearance. The whole surface will appear clear and shiny if properly adhered.

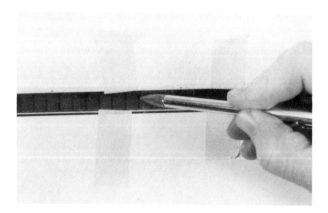

Step 7. Although it is possible to run the film through the projector with a tab on only one side of the film, a permanent, strong splice will result if a second tab is placed on the other side of the film. Remove the four pieces of masking tape holding the film down on the working surface. Turn the film over and replace the masking tape as described and discussed in Step 2. Remember to place the tape so it adheres to the edges of the film and does not extend into the picture area.

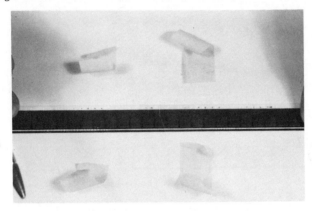

Step 8. Carefully place the splicing tab on this reverse side of the film following Steps 4 and 5, as discussed and illustrated above. Burnish the entire area of this second tab with a smooth, round object, being careful that the whole area is in good contact with the film, as discussed and illustrated in Step 6. Remove the four pieces of masking tape from the edges of the film. It is important to carefully, but thoroughly, clean away any sticky residue that may be left on the film.

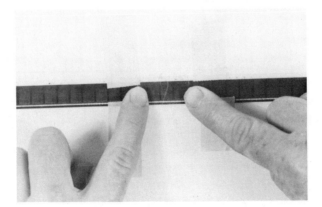

Appendix B

Using Theatrical Films in the Classroom

Theatrical feature films are motion picture films that are originally produced in 35mm or 70mm size and intended primarily for entertainment use in theaters. These feature films are photographically reduced to the standard classroom size of 16mm so that they can be projected on a regular classroom sound motion picture projector. Theatrical films, reduced to the 16mm format, are obtainable on either a rental or purchase basis. These films are widely available and provide the classroom teacher with a wealth of subject matter applicable and adaptable for student consumption in classroom instruction. Theatrical films are available in most subject disciplines taught in the public schools of America, subjects such as psychology, sociology, history, all areas of the humanities, physical education, science, etc.

Theatrical films bring to the classroom the best talent in the entertainment business. Such actors and actresses as Orson Wells, Vincent Price, Robert Redford, John Wayne, Spencer Tracy, Jane Fonda, and Julie Andrews (to name just a few) combine their talents with staged and actual location settings to vividly bring the "world-into-the-classroom."

The utilization of feature films for classroom study presents some special problems, not encountered with 16mm

educational films, that teachers must be aware of and prepare
for if they are to feel success with their use. These special
problems revolve about three basic areas:

1. Feature films, many times, deal with subject matter in
a superficial way. The script writer is not apt to dig beneath
the surface of the story and explain *why* people behave as
they do. Cause-and-effect is largely ignored; hence, the film's
superficiality becomes unrealistic.

Marriage and romance are treated superficially in theatrical films. Many movie-goers have come to accept the
theatrical film as an interpretation of real life. Young people
that view these films may not be able to sort out truth from
falsehood.

2. One of the far-reaching concerns, when independently
viewing and utilizing theatrical films in the classroom, is the
too-frequent method of portrayal of many of the values for
which Americans strive today. Far too often, theatrical films
portray the good life as the acquisitive life, with undue
emphasis on luxury, fine homes and automobiles, swank and
suavity, and urbane and super-sophisticated living. Influenced
by feature films and television, many young people graduate
from high school and immediately want all of the good life
they have seen and come to accept as "common." This
disparity between the theater-world and the real-world causes
much frustration.

3. The most pressing concern about theatrical films
centers on the degree and kind of influence that they have on
the attitudes and conduct of school children. Theatrical films
can introduce the child to and acquaint him or her with a
type of life which may have immediate, practical, and
momentous significance. These portrayed life styles may be
in direct conflict with the values, ethics, and purpose of other
educational institutions in the life of the child. The conflict-
ing forces can cause great turmoil in the minds of the young.
The schemes of conduct which these theatrical productions

present may not only fill gaps left by the school, the home, and the church, but also they may thwart the standards and values which the home, the church, and the school seek to inculcate. For the young movie-goer, little discrimination is possible.

Teachers have a two-fold responsibility to their students in the viewing of theatrical motion pictures. One concern is centered on the out-of-classroom viewing of the films, and the other is the classroom utilization of theatrical films. In regard to the first concern, teachers can do much to combat the problems inherent in these films by teaching children and students to discriminate and evaluate them. First, by developing an awareness of the effects of movies on individuals; second, helping children and young people to select the movies they attend more carefully and thoughtfully. Teachers could do well to devote several classroom study periods to the discussion of the inherent problems of theatrical movies.

There are many hundreds of theatrical films that can be utilized in classroom instruction—films that can make significant contributions not only to the basic knowledge of people, places, and things, but also to the development of the moral character of students as desired and emulated by the home, the church, and the school.

The use of theatrical films in classroom instruction places a heavy burden on the teacher in selecting, planning, and presenting the lesson phases as described in this text. Teachers must select the films with great care. They must be thoroughly previewed, and the objectionable, questionable, slanted, biased, untrue, etc., portions isolated for use in the introduction to the lesson. In presenting the objectives of the lesson to the students, these concerns will need to be listed, and alternatives to the objectionable issues must be advanced and discussed in detail. Students will need to have ample opportunities to discuss all sides of the issues presented in the film. This discussion will need to be directed by the teacher to be sure that misinterpretations, half-truths, and unfamiliar concepts are clarified and understood by the students.

Theatrical feature films are available from many sources on both a rental and purchase basis. Many of these sources are listed as follows:

ABC MEDIA CONCEPTS
1330 Avenue of the Americas
New York, New York 10019

ARGOSY FILM SERVICE
1939 Central Street
Evanston, Illinois 60201

CAROUSEL FILMS, INC.
1501 Broadway
New York, New York 10036

CINE WORLD-HURLOCK
13 Arcadia Road
Old Greenwich, Connecticut
    06870

CINECRAFT FILMS
1720 N.W. Marshall
P.O. Box 4126
Portland, Oregon 97208

CLEM WILLIAMS FILMS, INC.
2240 Noblestown Road
Pittsburgh, Pennsylvania 15205

COLUMBIA CINEMATHEQUE
711 Fifth Avenue
New York, New York 10022

DuPONT de NEMOURS & CO.
Motion Picture Section
1007 Market Street
Wilmington, Delaware 19898

EMGEE FILM LIBRARY
16024 Ventura Boulevard,
Suite 211
Encino, California 91436

FOCUS FILM PRODUCTIONS
1385 Westwood Boulevard
Los Angeles, California 90024

IMAGES
2 Purdy Avenue
Rye, New York 10580

IMPACT FILMS
144 Bleecker Street
New York, New York 10012

INSTITUTIONAL CINEMA,
    INC.
915 Broadway
New York, New York 10010

ISRAEL INFORMATION SER-
    VICES
11 East 70th Street
New York, New York 10021

IVY FILMS
165 West 46th Street
New York, New York 10036

JANUS FILMS
745 Fifth Avenue
New York, New York 10022

KIT PARKER FILMS
Carmel Valley, California 93924

MACMILLAN FILMS
c/o G B Media
333 North Flores Street
Los Angeles, California 90048

MANBECK PICTURES COR-
PORATION
3621 Wakonda Drive
Des Moines, Iowa 50321

CONTEMPORARY/MCGRAW-
HILL FILMS
1221 Avenue of the Americas
New York, New York 10020

MODERN SOUND PICTURES,
INC.
1402 Howard Street
Omaha, Nebraska 68102

MOTTAS FILMS, INC.
1318 Ohio Avenue, N.W.
Canton, Ohio 44705

THE MUSEUM OF MODERN
ART
11 West 53rd Street
New York, New York 10019

NATIONAL FILM SERVICE
14 Glenwood Avenue
Raleigh, North Carolina 17602

NEW YORKER FILMS
16 West 61st Street
New York, New York 10023

PARAMOUNT PICTURES
1 Gulf and Western Plaza
New York, New York 10023

REEL IMAGES
495 Monroe TPK
Monroe, Connecticut 06468

STERLING   EDUCATIONAL
FILMS
241 East 34th Street
New York, New York 10016

SWANK MOTION PICTURES,
INC.
6767 Forest Lawn Drive
Hollywood, California 90068
also
393 Front Street
Hempstead, New York 11550
also
1200 Roosevelt Road
Glen Ellyn, Illinois 60137

TRICONTINENTAL   FILM
CENTER
244 West 27th Street
New York, New York 10001

TWYMAN FILMS, INC.
329 Salem Avenue
Box 605
Dayton, Ohio 45401

UNITED ARTISTS CORPORA-
TION
2904 Woodburn Avenue
Cincinnati, Ohio 45206

UNIVERSAL 16
155 Universal City Plaza
Universal City, California 91608

V.C.I. FILMS
6555 East Skelly Drive
Tulsa, Oklahoma 74145

WALT DISNEY EDUCATION-
AL MEDIA COMPANY
500 South Buena Vista Street
Burbank, California 91521

WARNER BROS. FILM
GALLERY
400 Warner Boulevard
Burbank, California 91522

WESTCOAST FILMS
25 Lusk Street
San Francisco, California 94107

WORLD WIDE PICTURES
1313 Hennepin Avenue
Minneapolis, Minnesota 55403

About the Author

LaMond F. Beatty is Associate Professor in the department of Educational Systems and Learning Resources, Graduate School of Education, University of Utah, Salt Lake City, Utah. Dr. Beatty has taught at the University of Utah since 1961. Along with his teaching responsibilities, he has been the Assistant Director and Director (1961 through 1973) of the Educational Media Center for the University of Utah, helping to develop the Center from a small 16mm film rental and campus service agency to a Media Center that offers a 16mm film, photographic, and graphic service plus an instructional design unit utilized by instructors and administrators in all colleges of the University of Utah.

Dr. Beatty has published widely, including magazine articles, monographs, textbook chapters, manuals, independent study courses, and mini-textbooks.

Dr. Beatty maintains affiliations with both local and national professional organizations, including the Utah Educational Media Association (UEMA), the Utah Library Association (ULA), the Association for Educational Communications and Technology (AECT), Phi Delta Kappa, the American Library Association (ALA), and the Consortium of University Film Libraries.